BARRON'S DC

Boxers

Sharon Sakson

BARRON'S

Acknowledgments

The American Kennel Club's library of dog books proved invaluable for tracing Boxer history. Thanks to the AKC's director of communications Lisa Peterson, and AKC Vice President James Crowley for access to many excellent sources. The American Boxer Club provided essential literature, including information on health and breeding. Thanks to my mentors in the breed, longtime breeder and judges' education coordinator Stephanie Abraham and renowned Boxer breeder from Florida and Georgia, Alberto Berrios.

Max Magder contributed his vast knowledge. Yulia Lobova and Vadim Retsov introduced me to Russian and European Boxer breeders; Marilyn Tuesley provided introductions to English ones. Dr. Peter Batts (who is a Boxer owner himself) provided veterinary direction.

My brother, Drew Sakson, contributed a practical dog owner's point of view. Patti Fitzgerald was a great help with research. Gini Sikes and Gail Miller Bisher checked my grammar and spelling and made sure the sentences make sense. Chris Parsons provided extraordinary care for my dogs while the manuscript was being written.

Biggest help of all are my own dogs, Scout, Nessie, Vanyatta, Stella, Tassel, and Clarissa. Their enriching presence makes all the hard work worthwhile.

About the Author

Sharon Sakson is a journalist, writer, and television news producer. She raises puppies for assistance dog organizations and is an AKC dog show judge of Hound and Working breeds.

She has attended the American Boxer Club's National Specialty Show for many years, visited Boxer kennels, and attended seminars given by Boxer breeders. She has judged Boxers in England, Russia, Sweden, Finland, Taiwan, and Argentina. She is a contributing editor to *Dog News* and writes regularly for *Dogs in Review*, *Dog World*, and other canine publications.

Her home includes an elderly Boxer who was homeless before joining Sharon's family in Princeton, New Jersey. Sharon's passion is writing books about dogs. Her book *Paws & Effect: The Healing Power of Dogs* has topped bestselling dog book lists.

Her other books are *Paws to Protect: Dogs Saving Lives & Restoring Hope*, *Brussels Griffons: A Complete Pet Owner's Manual*, and *Paws & Reflect: A Special Bond Between Man and Dog*, co-authored with Neil Plakcy. Her radio show, *Paws & Effect* (*webtalkradio.net*), opens with barked greetings from Buddy, her sister's Boxer.

All information and advice contained in this book has been reviewed by a veterinarian.

Cover Credits

Jeanmfogle.com: front cover; Tara Darling: back cover.

Photo Credits

Barbara Augello: pages vi, 98, 166; Seth Casteel: pages 2, 8, 11, 17, 22, 24, 39, 43, 68, 70, 116; Dreamstime: page 82; Cheryl Ertelt: page 125; Jeanmfogle.com: pages 5, 59, 60, 74, 149; Tracy Hendrickson: pages 37, 79, 94, 129, 131; iStockphoto: pages 26, 91, 115, 126, 165; Daniel Johnson/Paulette Johnson: pages 81, 134 (top and bottom), 135 (top and bottom), 136 (top and bottom), 137 (top and bottom), 138 (top and bottom), 139 (top and bottom), 143; Liz Kaye: page: 152; Lisa Kruss: pages 29, 47, 56, 76, 89; Kim Levin: page 13; Modern Life Photo: page 83; Oh My Dog! Photography: page i; Penzi Pet Photography: pages 14, 54; Laura Rogers Canine Photography: pages 18, 72, 113, 123; Sherpa Pet Group, LLC: page 20; Shutterstock: pages iii, 30, 33, 34, 41, 44, 69, 101, 107, 110, 119, 121, 132, 140, 159, 161, 162, 170; Connie Summers/Paulette Johnson: pages v, 4, 48, 53, 63, 84; Joan Hustace Walker: pages 58, 92, 103, 145, 146, 147, 148, 155.

All inquiries should be addressed to:
Barron's Educational Series, Inc.
250 Wireless Boulevard
Hauppauge, New York 11788
www.barronseduc.com

ISBN: 978-0-7641-4490-5 (Book)
ISBN: 978-0-7641-8678-3 (DVD)
ISBN: 978-0-7641-9770-3 (Package)

Library of Congress Catalog Card No: 2010008030

Library of Congress Cataloging-in-Publication Data

Sakson, Sharon R.
    Boxers / Sharon Sakson.
        p. cm. — (Barron's dog bibles)
    Includes index.
    ISBN-13: 978-0-7641-4490-5
    ISBN-10: 0-7641-4490-1
    1. Boxer (Dog breed) I. Title.
    SF429.B75S35 2010
    636.73—dc22   2010008030

Printed in China

9 8 7 6 5 4 3 2 1

CONTENTS

CONTENTS

As a longtime admirer of Boxers, I've spent a lot of time in their presence. As a Boxer friend, I admire their joyful spirit and precocious intelligence. As a dog show judge, I admire their efficient construction, strong necks, and springy, flexible gait.

Boxer owners have achievements to brag about in every area of dog competition and service, including assistance dogs, therapy dogs, and search and rescue. Boxers are wonderful friends and companions, and I'm proud to know them.

My favorite part of writing a book is researching it. I spent long hours in the library at the American Kennel Club offices in New York, turning the crackling old pages of Boxer magazines and books from the past. All around, paintings of dogs by distinguished artists looked on solemnly. The books revealed that the Boxer was a breed of honor in both World Wars, working as a guard, messenger, sentry, lookout, and escort, leading medics to badly injured soldiers.

Few stories in the dog world are as suspenseful as Friederun Stockmann's account of hiding and caring for her dogs while World War I and then World War II raged around her in Munich. Known as the "mother of the breed," she lived up to that title by ensuring that Boxer bloodlines survived the wars to become a favorite breed for families and children everywhere.

My research took me into the homes of breeders, where I learned that the Boxer is generally an easy whelper and good mother to her pups, which can number from four to ten.

Dog show exhibitors talk of the Boxer's love for the ring. A natural showoff, he considers it only right that all the spectators' attention should fall on him. Handlers cheer and applaud their dogs in the ring even when the Best of Breed ribbon goes to someone else, to reward the dogs for a valiant effort.

Parents told the same story again and again: The Boxer is unparalleled as a watchdog and a nanny. Boxers are known to prevent strangers, even the babysitter or a neighbor, from touching the children in their care until the parents convince them that it's okay.

In short, the Boxer personality is exciting and loving, heroic and down-to-earth. The breed is beloved by all who come to know it. In these pages, you will learn why.

Chapter One

All About Boxers

Boxers are loving, strong, exuberant, and protective dogs with a particular affinity for children. Their hearing is especially sharp, making them constantly alert to any danger; they're the self-appointed guardians of the home and family. Highly intelligent, they are able to recognize that most people and dogs who approach are not dangerous, but they always glance at their owners for acknowledgment that everything is okay.

Boxers are lovely to look at, with their smooth muscles, athletic grace, and noble bearing. There is a spring in their step when they move, whether after a tennis ball or keeping up with an excited child. Such characteristics explain their popularity and presence in family homes for the past 100 years. Currently, they rank sixth in popularity of the 163 breeds recognized by the American Kennel Club. They are the second most popular breed in Baltimore, Cincinnati, Des Moines, Louisville, Omaha, and Kansas City, and the third most popular breed in Atlanta, Cleveland, New Orleans, Minneapolis-St. Paul, Pittsburgh, St. Louis, and Philadelphia.

When Boxer owners get together, they immediately start swapping stories of their dogs' goofy antics. Well-raised Boxers are never hesitant or shy. They are natural clowns who quickly learn how to make their owners laugh. They will chase a favorite ball around and around on the floor, often boxing at it with their paws. They will hide their best-loved toys and bring them out when they're bored. They often are extremely attached to certain toys, carrying the same toy around and guarding it from everyone else for years.

Boxers are also curious dogs who like to investigate everything that goes on in their environment. When intrigued, they gaze intently at what is puzzling them. The look on their faces seems to say, "What is *that*? I'd really like to know."

Boxers are independent thinkers who are sometimes described as stubborn. They're not always motivated by stubbornness, however. They like to understand what you want and *why* you want them to do it—if they can be convinced that there's a good reason to get off the sofa, go outdoors, or perform whatever the task may be, they will do it.

Your Boxer will be happiest when everyone in the family is home and in the same room. Then he can travel from person to person, touching each one with his muzzle or his paw to let them know he cares, and accept a pat on the head or stroke across the back.

Fun Facts: Popularity

The Boxer is the most popular breed registered in the AKC Working Group, ahead of Rottweilers, Doberman Pinschers, and Great Danes.

Because of their affectionate nature, mature Boxers can be excellent therapy dogs, happy to visit with people who are sick. A young Boxer may be a little too enthusiastic for a hospital or nursing home environment, where it's important to remain calm and not bump into anyone—a lot to ask of ebullient young dogs. But once they reach adulthood, Boxers are capable of great restraint. They realize they have to be careful around the elderly or sick.

The breed is extremely sensitive to the moods and needs of humans. It is touching to see therapy Boxers in the pediatric ward or on the hospice floor, gently laying their heads on the knee of a patient. They seem to know that their presence can be healing and want to help in any way they can.

Although not water dogs by nature, Boxers are powerful swimmers who will often jump into the pool or lake with their human families.

Boxers are naturally clean and, therefore, easy to housetrain. They want to keep their living area unsoiled and will respond to positive teaching methods, but they will shut down and ignore you if they feel rushed or bullied.

Boxers generally have a strong food drive; they will sit or shake paws endlessly if there is a treat on hand as a reward. When the training is varied enough to keep them interested, they have proven to be excellent in obedience and rally competitions.

Boxers love the sport of agility, particularly when it comes to flying over hurdles and whipping through tunnels. They are flexible athletes who love to show off by lunging through the obstacles as fast as possible.

Many families acquire Boxers because of their well-known love of children. When there are children in the family, Boxers are instinctive guardians, happily taking on the role of nanny. Take the story of the couple who left their baby at home with a grandmother while they went to relax at a movie. Soon, the mother's cell phone was ringing with an urgent message to hurry back to the house. Their Boxer had decided that, since he didn't know the grandmother very well, she could not enter the baby's room. The parents thanked the dog for his concern but showed him that they trusted the grandmother. Once she had fed and rocked the baby in the parents' presence, everything was fine. The Boxer allowed the grandmother to take over while the parents caught the late show.

In a recent news article, a Boxer was credited with sounding the alarm when a nighttime fire threatened to engulf a home. He jumped on the bed where the parents were sleeping, refusing to get off or to calm down until they got up to check what was wrong. His action saved the family's lives.

A Boxer is a consistent character—he never ceases to protect his family in every way he can. Their safety is his foremost concern.

Characteristics of Boxers

Boxers are identified the world over by their unique head and outline. The distinctive square skull and jaw, upturned nose, wrinkled forehead, and big, dark eyes give the Boxer a look different from any other breed.

Breeders and dog show judges describe the Boxer as having square proportions, meaning that the body is approximately the same distance from chest to tail as from shoulder to floor. The head is squared off rather than rounded, like a Chihuahua, or long and wedge-shaped, like a Doberman Pinscher. Their upturned jaw lends Boxers their set and determined appearance. The Boxer's bearing is alert, dignified, and self-assured. In the show ring, his presence is one of constrained animation.

Boxers usually have a dry mouth, which means that they don't drool excessively, the way that St. Bernards or Bullmastiffs do. But steer clear of him when he's been drinking water—he often dribbles across the kitchen floor or shakes his head, sending water flying in every direction.

Boxers can be registered with the American Kennel Club in three colors—fawn, brindle, and white. The fawn shade can vary from light tan to dark mahogany. The brindle ranges from just a few sparse black brindle stripes on a fawn background to a heavy concentration of black.

Although white Boxers can be AKC registered, they are disqualified in the show ring if white markings exceed one-third of the coat. But white Boxers make equally good pets and family members as their fawn and brindle cousins.

Boxers have black masks, usually with white markings, such as a blaze down the forehead, a white chest, or white socks.

The tight, square body of the Boxer reminds the observer of a prize-fighter, the athlete from whom he gets his name. On the website of the American Kennel Club, the Boxer is described as "the well-conditioned middleweight athlete of dogdom."

This canine, however, is anything but a pugilist in demeanor. Owners' home videos show Boxers lying next to small children who swat at them, bite their tails, take their toys, and pinch their toes. Another breed might yowl, bark, and nip when bothered by children, but Boxers remain unperturbed and calm. No matter how much the kids roughhouse with them, they are completely devoted to their small charges, as evidenced by home videos of Boxers guarding baby carriages and pulling children back to the house by their clothing.

Every day, Boxer owners upload dozens of photographs and videos on the Internet that offer a visual picture of the Boxer personality. There are photos of Boxers meeting cats, investigating trash containers, and chasing frogs. There are Boxers staring in fascination at animal programs on TV. More than any other breed, Boxers seem to love bouncing on trampolines. Trampolines exaggerate the Boxer's love of jumping and naturally exuberant personality. You'll find videos of Boxers being pitched high into the air!

When he's not outside being athletic, he can usually be found inside on his favorite bed, one eye open to see what family members are up to. One of the most endearing Boxer characteristics is how strongly he bonds with those he loves. In an increasingly technology-driven culture, the Boxer offers a strong connection to the natural world. He loves fully and openly, which is why he can be easily hurt with a sharp word. He is often able to bring out the best in his human companions, prompting us to love, nurture, feel tenderness, and act on our best intentions. Your Boxer has the potential to bring out the best in you.

The History of Boxers

The Boxer is a descendant of two European dog breeds that no longer exist, the Danziger Bullenbaisser and the Brabenter Bullenbeisser. Bullenbeisser means "bull biter." The history of the breed reflects the cruel behavior of humans toward animals in past decades. In the Boxer's case, the cruelty was based on the belief in the Middle Ages that the meat of a bull was tough and indigestible unless he was "baited," or harassed, tormented, and teased just before slaughter. The bull was tied on about fifteen feet of chain from a stake in the ground to a collar around his neck. The butcher brought in his bullenbeisser, urging the dog to attack and bite the bull.

The enraged bull couldn't get away, so he tried desperately to hook the dog with his horn. When he did, he would toss the body into the air, sometimes as high as 30 feet. In 1719, one spectator, M. Misson, wrote that the bull's goal is "to throw him so high in the air that he may break his neck in the fall. To avoid this danger, the dog's friends are ready beneath him, some with their backs, to give him a soft reception; and others with long poles, which they offer him slantways, to the intent that, sliding down them, it may break the force of his fall."

This practice required a strong dog with a broad, powerful jaw to hold onto the bull. German butchers used giant molossers, mastiff-type dogs that had populated Europe since the Romans marched through it. These huge dogs were very highly valued, not only for their bullbaiting abilities but also as hunters of big game, such as deer, bear, wild boar, and bison.

In England, traveling Germans acquired smaller bulldogs and shorthaired terriers. They bred them to their mastiffs to increase the dogs' tenacity and fearlessness. The result of this cross was the bullenbeisser.

The nose of the bullenbeisser tilted slightly back, a modification that allowed the dog to breathe through his nostrils even while his jaws remained clamped on the bull. This structure has carried through to the Boxer of today.

The belief that it was necessary to bait a bull before slaughtering was so pervasive that, in England in the 1600s, it was a crime to sell "un-baited" bull meat. Court records from 1612 recount that Michael Alford of Somerset and five other butchers were convicted and fined for the offense of not baiting their bulls before slaughtering them. The enraged clients felt that they had been sold tough beef.

The Middle Ages looked on bullbaiting and bearbaiting as great entertainment. Both royalty and working-class citizens attended baiting events. Crowds cheered on the dogs as they tormented and then killed the bull, bear, or other wild animal. *The Dog Fancier's Companion*, a book published in 1819, noted that a bullbaiting or bearbaiting dog is "…the fiercest of all dog kind, and is probably the most courageous creature in the world. Its courage in attacking the bull is well known; its fury in seizing, and its invincible obstinacy in maintaining its hold is truly astonishing."

By the 1800s, it had been clearly established that baiting bulls did not make meat any more tender. There was growing awareness that violence toward animals was cruel and uncivilized. The blood sports of bullbaiting and dog fighting slowly lost favor.

A bill banning these practices was introduced into the British House of Commons in 1802, but it took 33 years to get enough votes to pass. It finally became law in 1835. Most countries passed similar laws during that period. While bullbaiting disappeared, dogfighting unfortunately went underground and continues as an illegal sport today.

FYI: How the Boxer Got His Name

The name *Boxer* dates from the 1800s. The first published appearance was in 1845, in Charles Dickens's novella *The Cricket on the Hearth*. (The main character, John Peerybingle, has a dog named Boxer.)

A group of dogs known as *bierboxers* were bred in Munich in the 1800s, according to the canine researcher Milo Denlinger. Perhaps the Boxer took his name from them. Dogs who worked with butchers, helping to hold bulls for slaughter, were known as *boxl*, another possible source of the name.

But the theory heard most often is that the Germans used the anglicized word *boxer*, meaning pugilist or prizefighter, because a breed characteristic of Boxers is that they use their paws to punch and play in a manner that brings to mind two men fighting in a ring. Boxer owners are constantly entertained by the sight of their Boxers standing on their hind legs and batting at other dogs in play. Perhaps that's why Rocky Balboa's breed of choice was the Boxer in the movie series *Rocky*.

Even though they no longer needed strong dogs to bait bulls, German butchers still found their bullenbeissers very useful. They helped with managing cattle in slaughter yards and proved themselves great guardians of the home. These "butchers' dogs" began to be valued for their intelligence, loyalty, and devotion to children. Dogs with those qualities were bred to each other, establishing the smart and tractable personality of the breed.

The Boxer Breed Is Born

In 1894, three German breeders decided to work together to establish the Boxer breed. A Boxer was entered in a dog show for the first time in Munich in 1895. She was Mühlbauer's Flocki owned by George Alt, the result of a mating between the Boxer Alt's Schecken with a Bulldog named Dr. Toneissen's Tom.

In 1896, German Boxer breeders founded the Deutscher Boxer Club. Members wrote a detailed standard describing the breed, which was published in 1902. It has undergone only minor revisions from that time to the current day.

Around the turn of the century, the German military conscripted Boxers, putting their bravery and eagerness to help to use. They performed the roles of messenger, guard, and sentry, and they were sent out to lead medics to injured soldiers who were still alive but hiding on the battlefield from the enemy. These men surely would have died if the canine scouts had not found them. When the wars were over, police used Boxers in their work for patrolling, guarding, and subduing criminals.

Boxers were part of the canine corps in World War II. They were perfect for the job except for one thing; their extremely short coat does not provide

protection from the cold nor insulation from heat. Additionally, the Boxer's short muzzle makes it hard for them to keep cool in hot weather, so they are prone to excessive panting and overheating.

Because of the Boxer's sensitivity to temperature, German Shepherds and Rottweilers became the military dogs of choice. Boxer breeding since that time has concentrated on the amiable qualities of the breed rather than the ferocious ones. The modern Boxer emerged as a strong, smart, agile companion and guard.

The breeder of the Vom Dom Boxers, Friederun Stockmann, related in her memoir that she was able to earn enough money to keep alive during both World Wars by selling Boxer puppies to American GIs. Like all German men, her husband, Captain Philip Stockmann, was required to fight. He died in a concentration camp while waiting for his name to be cleared so he could return to his beloved wife and kennel. He had taken six Boxers with him into Hitler's army as war dogs. All six perished at the front.

Fortunately, Friederun Stockmann was able to save enough Boxers to continue the line. The Boxers she sold to Americans were instrumental in carrying forward the beautiful type and personality characteristics of Vom Doms, giving the breed a good start in the United States.

Boxers in the United States

The first Boxer registered by the American Kennel Club was Arnulf Grandenz, born in 1904 from U.S. parents who had been imported from Germany. Arnulf was bred and owned by Max H. Schachner in Downers

Grove, Illinois. The first Boxer to win a championship was the imported German Sieger Dampf Vom Dom, in 1915, imported from the Vom Dom kennel, the world-famous line of German Boxers in the early years of the breed. The first Boxer to win Best in Show in the United States was German Sieger Champion Check v. Hunnenstein in 1932.

The breed grew in popularity in the late 1930s through the 1950s, but, as part of the normal cycle of a breed's ups and downs, declined in the 1970s while German Shepherds, Poodles, and other breeds snagged center stage. In 1980, Boxers' popularity slowly started to rise again. The breed reentered the AKC's top ten most popular breeds in 2000 and remains in the top ten today, a great testament to the Boxer's wonderful personality.

The Trendsetting Ambassador for the Breed

There is only one candidate for the title Greatest Boxer of the 20th Century—Champion Bang Away of Sirrah Crest. Bang Away was an important winner and sire in the dog show world. But his influence was even more important to the dog-loving public at large. Many people who had never seen a Boxer before learned about them by reading about Bang Away in magazines and newspapers. He was a superstar celebrity of his era.

Bang Away was born on February 17, 1949, in California, at the home of Dr. R. C. and Phoebe Harris. When the venerable Frau Stockmann came from Germany to judge a Boxer club match show, she saw the four-month-old Bang Away and awarded him Best in Match. "He is the best Boxer in America," she told the spectators. She predicted that Bang Away would have a major influence on Boxers in the United States.

Her prediction quickly came true. In 1951, Bang Away won Best in Show at the Westminster Kennel Club Dog Show. His owner, Mrs. Harris, remembers that during Bang Away's career, there were only four judges who failed to acknowledge him as Best of Breed. (Two of those later repented by awarding him Best in Show.) The crowd threw chairs and bottles and booed one of the judges. Police had to be called to escort the judge from the building—a very unusual occurrence at a dog show, which is usually quiet and formal, and where polite good sportsmanship is the norm. But the crowd was right; it was later discovered that the judge had been paid off to keep the win from Bang Away, and he was disbarred from ever judging again.

Bang Away went on to win an amazing 121 Bests in Show from 1951 to 1956. Fewer than 25 dogs of any breed have ever won more than one hundred AKC Bests in Show, even now, when there are 5,000 dog shows held each year!

The heyday of Boxers in the show ring was from 1946 to 1956, when they were often the largest entry at the show. Boxers won the majority of the Working Group titles, as Bang Away kept piling up his Best in Show wins.

Bang Away changed the look of American Boxers. Before Bang Away, American Boxers were cobby, substantial, and carried heavy bone. Bang Away was taller, more elegant and streamlined, and carried himself with a great deal of flair. He initiated the look we see in the Boxer breed today.

As a sire, Bang Away was responsible for producing 81 champions, a record that still stands, more than fifty years later.

One of the presidents of the American Boxer Club, John Connolly, recalled, "When he was in the ring you could not take your eyes off him, you couldn't look at anything else." Prizes were different in those days; Connolly recalled that for one particular Best in Show, Bang Away won a large washing machine! These days, the reward is more likely to be a huge rosette and *possibly* a small gift, like a canvas camp chair or a bag to carry grooming supplies.

Bang Away was the subject of stories in *Vanity Fair, Collier's, Esquire, Life, Sports Illustrated,* and *Time* magazines. Wherever he went, newspaper photographers rushed to snap his picture. Connolly recalled that on his airline journeys, pilots asked Bang Away to come up and ride in the cockpit. A great showman, Bang Away loved the attention.

He became a tremendous ambassador for the breed. It seemed that everyone who saw him wanted a Boxer, and Boxer breeding flourished. In the years since, no one Boxer has ever succeeded in cap- turing the public spotlight the way Bang Away did in the 1950s.

Why You Want a Boxer

There are many reasons why you want a Boxer. That lovely Boxer expression. The way his forehead wrinkles when he's curious. His unwavering devotion. The happy way he greets the day. His refusal to take life too seriously. His sense of humor. His superb guarding qualities.

But a Boxer is not the right dog for everyone. You and a Boxer will not be suited for each other if any of the following are true:

- You don't have room for a big dog. The Boxer is generally about 23 to 25 inches tall at the shoulder and weighs about 55 to 70 pounds. Although described as medium in size, he is big enough to bump into furniture, knock over small tables, and steal food from the kitchen counter.

Fun Facts

Boxer Popularity

Boxers are among the most popular breeds in England and the United States. The breed has ranked among the top ten most popular breeds in American Kennel Club registrations for many years, and today it stands as the sixth most popular breed in America.

While Boxers retain popularity nationally, the following several big cities don't place them in the top ten: New York, Los Angeles, Detroit, Miami, Portland (Oregon), San Diego, San Francisco, Seattle, and Honolulu.

The Boxer's ranking over the years*

2009	6	2004	7
2008	6	1999	10
2006	7	1995	15

*according to AKC registration statistics

- You don't like exercise. A Boxer needs your help to get adequate exercise, whether it's throwing a ball in the backyard or taking him on long walks. Some Boxer owners have their dogs jump on trampolines or swim in the pool. Adequate exercise is key for having a well-mannered dog.
- You don't have time to train him. Boxers are not born knowing the house rules; they need to be taught. Young Boxers need discipline in order to heed your requests to stop jumping or lunging and walk quietly on a leash.
- You don't like a dog in the house. A Boxer's short coat affords him little insulation from the heat or cold. He is a house dog who needs to be near his human family, where he can give and take affection. He will not thrive if left outdoors.
- You don't like puppy behavior. Boxers are slow to mature! Some are still as boisterous and happy as puppies when they are three or four years old. Even though they are adults, some will still run off with one of your shoes or hide a dropped fork, just because they think it's funny.
- You can't stand drooling and snoring. This varies with individual dogs. As mentioned earlier, some Boxers slobber. Some may also snore. Don't get a Boxer if you can't live with even moderate drooling or snoring.
- You hate even a small amount of shedding. Boxers have very short coats, but they do shed about twice a year, when the weather changes. Daily brushing will help remove dead hair, but you will still see hairs, particularly the white ones, on your car seat, furniture, and clothing.

- You don't want your dog to be smarter than you. While Boxers are intelligent and respond well to training, their brains work overtime to come up with ways to outsmart you.
- You want a dog who will only do what you say. Boxers have their own busy minds. They are willing to work with you but unwilling to be roughly ordered around.
- You don't have a sense of humor. Boxers have a tendency to act goofy. They will try to capture the beam of a flashlight or pretend they don't know where their toy is. They will chase a fly off your leg, watch traffic and pedestrians going by, or grumble deep in their throats as if trying to talk to you.

You want a Boxer if your taste runs toward medium-sized, heavily built dogs with short, tight-fitting coats. You want a Boxer if you like his tuxedo look, his chiseled head, and his powerful muscles. You want a Boxer if you would enjoy a fellow hiker or jogger who is always ready to go. You want a Boxer if you could use a watchful guard around the house, if you are single and need a friend, or if you have a family and need a protector. A properly trained Boxer is the perfect companion.

The only question is, are you worthy of his allegiance? He is going to be your partner, your friend, and your soul mate. You owe it to him to provide the best care.

Blueprint for a Boxer

The Boxer is considered a member of the Working Group by the American Kennel Club. The following is the standard for the breed, approved by the American Boxer Club, which is known to its members as ABC.

General Appearance

The ideal Boxer is a medium-sized, square-built dog of good substance with short back, strong limbs, and short, tight-fitting coat. His well-developed muscles are clean, hard, and appear smooth under taut skin. His movements denote energy. The gait is firm yet elastic, the stride free and ground-covering, and the carriage proud. Developed to serve as guard, working, and companion dog, he combines strength and agility with elegance and style. His expression is alert and his temperament steadfast and tractable.

The chiseled head imparts to the Boxer a unique individual stamp. It must be in correct proportion to the body. The broad, blunt muzzle is the distinctive feature, and great value is placed upon its being of proper form and balance with the skull.

In judging the Boxer, first consideration is given to general appearance and overall balance. Special attention is then devoted to the head, after which the individual body components are examined for their correct construction, and the gait evaluated for efficiency.

Size
Adult males 23 to 25 inches; females 21½ to 23½ inches at the withers. Proper balance and quality in the individual should be of primary importance since there is no size disqualification.

Proportion
The body in profile is square in that a horizontal line from the front of the forechest to the rear projection of the upper thigh should equal the length of a vertical line dropped from the top of the withers to the ground.

Substance
Sturdy, with balanced musculature. Males larger boned than females.

Head
The beauty of the head depends upon the harmonious proportion of muzzle to skull. The blunt muzzle is one-third the length of the head from the occiput to the tip of the nose, and two-thirds the width of the skull. The head should be clean, not showing deep wrinkles (wet). Wrinkles typically appear upon the forehead when ears are erect, and are always present from the lower edge of the stop running downward on both sides of the muzzle.

Expression
Intelligent and alert.

Eyes
Dark brown in color, frontally placed, generous, not too small, too protruding, or too deep-set. Their mood-mirroring character, combined with the wrinkling of the forehead, gives the Boxer head its unique quality of expressiveness. Third eyelids preferably have pigmented rims.

Ears

Set at the highest points of the sides of the skull, the ears are customarily cropped, cut rather long and tapering, and raised when alert. If uncropped, the ears should be of moderate size, thin, lying flat and close to the cheeks in repose, but falling forward with a definite crease when alert.

Skull

The top of the skull is slightly arched, not rounded, flat, nor noticeably broad, with the occiput not overly pronounced. The forehead shows a slight indentation between the eyes and forms a distinct stop with the topline of the muzzle. The cheeks should be relatively flat and not bulge (cheekiness), maintaining the clean lines of the skull as they taper into the muzzle in a slight, graceful curve.

Muzzle and Nose

The muzzle, proportionately developed in length, width, and depth, has a shape influenced first through the formation of both jawbones, second through the placement of the teeth, and third through the texture of the lips. The top of the muzzle should not slant down (downfaced), nor should it be concave (dishfaced); however, the tip of the nose should lie slightly higher than the root of the muzzle. The nose should be broad and black.

Fun Facts

The Boxer has particularly acute hearing. When you see him cock his head to the side and look puzzled, it is because he has picked up sounds too low or distant for your human hearing. He relies on this hearing while on guard duty.

Bite and Jaw Structure

The Boxer bite is undershot, the lower jaw protruding beyond the upper and curving slightly upward. The incisor teeth of the lower jaw are in a straight line, with the canines preferably up front in the same line to give the jaw the greatest possible width. The upper line of the incisors is slightly convex with the corner upper incisors fitting snugly in back of the lower canine teeth on each side. Neither the teeth nor the tongue should ever show when the mouth is closed.

The upper jaw is broad where attached to the skull and maintains this breadth, except for a very slight tapering to the front. The lips, which complete the formation of the muzzle, should meet evenly in front. The upper lip is thick and padded, filling out the frontal space created by the projection of the lower jaw, and laterally is supported by the canines of the lower jaw. Therefore, these canines must stand far apart and be of good length so that the front surface of the muzzle is broad and squarish and, when viewed from the side, shows moderate layback. The chin should be perceptible from the side as well as from the front. Any suggestion of an overlip obscuring the chin should be penalized.

Neck

Round, of ample length, muscular and clean without excessive hanging skin (dewlap). The neck should have a distinctly arched and elegant nape blending smoothly into the withers.

Back and Topline

The back is short, straight, muscular, firm, and smooth. The topline is slightly sloping when the Boxer is at attention, leveling out when in motion.

Body

The chest is of fair width, and the forechest well-defined and visible from the side. The brisket is deep, reaching down to the elbows; the depth of the body at the lowest point of the brisket equals half the height of the dog at the withers. The ribs, extending far to the rear, are well-arched but not barrel-shaped.

Breed Truths

Boxers are brachycephalic, which means they have a relatively broad, short skull and a short muzzle. They are prognathous, which means the lower jaw protrudes beyond the upper jaw and curves slightly upward. Their teeth align in an underbite, which means the lower teeth are in front of the upper teeth. This construction gives the Boxer a powerful bite, which in years past he used to hold onto large prey.

The loins are short and muscular. The lower stomach line is slightly tucked up, blending into a graceful curve to the rear. The croup is slightly sloped, flat and broad. The pelvis is long, and in females especially broad. The tail is set high, docked, and carried upward. An undocked tail should be severely penalized.

Forequarters

The shoulders are long and sloping, close-lying, and not excessively covered with muscle (loaded). The upper arm is long, approaching a right angle to the shoulder blade. The elbows should not press too closely to the chest wall nor stand off visibly from it. The forelegs are long, straight, and firmly muscled, and, when viewed from the front, stand parallel to each other. The pastern is strong and distinct, slightly slanting, but standing almost perpendicular to the ground. The dewclaws may be removed. Feet should be compact, turning neither in nor out, with well-arched toes.

Hindquarters

The hindquarters are strongly muscled, with angulation in balance with that of the forequarters. The thighs are broad and curved, the breech musculature hard and strongly developed. Upper and lower thigh are long. The legs are well-angulated at the stifle, neither too steep nor over-angulated, with clearly defined, well "let down" hock joints. Viewed from behind, the hind legs should be straight, with hock joints leaning neither in nor out. From the side, the leg below the hock (metatarsus) should be almost perpendicular to the ground, with a slight slope to the rear permissible. The metatarsus should be short, clean, and strong. The Boxer has no rear dewclaws.

Coat

Short, shiny, lying smooth and tight to the body.

Color

The colors are fawn and brindle. Fawn shades vary from light tan to mahogany. The brindle ranges from sparse but clearly defined black stripes on a fawn background to such a heavy concentration of black striping that the essential fawn background color barely, although clearly, shows through (which may create the appearance of reverse brindling). White markings, if present, should be of such distribution as to enhance the dog's appearance, but may not exceed one-third of the entire coat. They are not desirable on the flanks or on the back of the torso proper. On the face, white may replace part of the otherwise essential black mask, and may extend in an upward path between the eyes, but it must not be excessive, so as to detract from true Boxer expression. The absence of white markings, the "plain" fawn or brindle, is perfectly acceptable, and should not be penalized in any consideration of color.

Gait

Viewed from the side, proper front and rear angulation is manifested in a smoothly efficient, level-backed, ground-covering stride with a powerful drive emanating from a freely operating rear. Although the front legs do not contribute impelling power, adequate reach should be evident to prevent interference, overlap, or sidewinding (crabbing). Viewed from the front, the shoulders should remain trim and the elbows not flare out. The legs are

parallel until gaiting narrows the track in proportion to increasing speed, then the legs come in under the body but should never cross. The line from the shoulder down through the leg should remain straight although not necessarily perpendicular to the ground. Viewed from the rear, a Boxer's rump should not roll. The hind feet should dig in and track relatively true with the front. Again, as speed increases, the normally broad rear track will become narrower. The Boxer's gait should always appear smooth and powerful, never stilted or inefficient.

Character and Temperament

These are of paramount importance in the Boxer. Instinctively a hearing guard dog, his bearing is alert, dignified, and self-assured. In the show ring, his behavior should exhibit constrained animation. With family and friends, his temperament is fundamentally playful, yet patient and stoical with children. Deliberate and wary with strangers, he will exhibit curiosity, but, most importantly, fearless courage if threatened. However, he responds promptly to friendly overtures that are honestly rendered. His intelligence, loyal affection, and tractability to discipline make him a highly desirable companion. Any evidence of shyness, or lack of dignity or alertness, should be severely penalized.

The foregoing description is that of the ideal Boxer. Any deviation from the above-described dog must be penalized to the extent of the deviation.

Disqualifications

Boxers that are any color other than fawn or brindle. Boxers with a total of white markings exceeding one-third of the entire coat.

Chapter Two

The Mind
of the Boxer

The Boxer is fundamentally a playful, alert dog who exhibits great patience and tolerance with children. He is wary of strangers but quick to accept them if his family approves. He exhibits a great deal of curiosity. He is fearless and brave if his family or home is threatened. The Boxer is intelligent, loyal, affectionate, and tractable. Properly trained, he listens well and is a highly desirable companion.

Innate Behaviors of Boxers

The Boxer is a naturally clean dog, which makes him easy to housetrain. He does not like to soil his home. He is cooperative with the housetraining process.

Boxers are happy to be the only dog in the house. They can be extremely jealous of any other dog or cat who wants to share the family's affection.

Boxers are problem solvers. They can be very clever, particularly when it comes to obtaining food. They can swipe a ham sandwich off a kitchen counter in seconds if you are not looking, and they have been known to devour entire birthday cakes. The best thing to do if such a situation arises is to treat it as a training exercise. You're lucky if you catch him in the act, because you can say, "No! That's bad!"

Trainers sometimes say that if you don't catch your dog in the act, you can't reprimand him because he won't understand what you want. But this isn't true with Boxers. Boxers are smart and sensitive. Your Boxer knows what he did wrong. If he didn't, he would simply take your sandwiches right out of your hand. Point to the counter or show him the empty cake box and tell him, "You were bad. A bad dog did this."

He will know from your tone exactly what you are saying. His expression and body language will tell you how he feels about it. In most cases, he will look guilty and lower his head. Young Boxers may pretend they don't hear you and try to get you to play. You don't have to punish him further; your reaction is enough. He'll know that he shouldn't do that again. Training is a matter of consistency and repetition. If he steals the sandwich and you say nothing, he has taught himself that it's okay to do it when you are not looking.

A Boxer is capable of fending for himself during the day while you are at work. But when you come home, he lets you know in the most exuberant way that this is the highlight of his day, the moment he has been waiting for. Your Boxer will make you understand that he considers you special, wonderful, extraordinary, and superior to all other humans on earth.

Your Boxer is happiest when you're at home, even if you do something boring, like watching sports on television or making dinner. A Boxer can't be left in the backyard and visited only occasionally. He is a house dog. Only in the heart of the family will he flourish.

Boxers do not do well in extreme heat or extreme cold. On those days, his potty trips will be quick. He will dash out for a pee and seconds later be at the back door, anxious to come in.

Boxers love toys. Pet stores are full of toys, but this dog requires the most tough and durable ones. The Kong is a good choice. It bounces when dropped, and Boxers love to chew the rubber compound. Even better, stuff it with food or treats to keep him busy for a long time. While chewing his Kong, he can't get into trouble destroying your furniture. Tennis balls, big

rubber balls, Nylabones, dental chews, big biscuits, rope toys, rolled-up towels, and stuffed teddy bears will all make your Boxer happy.

The Merry Prankster

Boxers are natural comedians. They delight in stealing and hiding a sock, and then watching you search for it. Like children, they practice a form of selective deafness. They respond when you say, "Want a cookie?" or "Time for dinner!" But their hearing fails them when you say, "Please get off my chair," or "You have to go in your crate now."

They are likely to look surprised when you wake them. But if *you* sleep too soundly when your Boxer wants to get up, he may well pounce on you or slurp your face with his thick, giant tongue.

Some Boxers like to watch television. One Boxer owner swears that her Boxer is glued to the set when dog shows come on, and he gets excited when he spies another Boxer in the ring.

The Boxer enjoys his role as class clown. He has a wide range of animated facial expressions and quickly learns which get a laugh. But probably his best trick is simply to lay his head on your knee, gazing up at you with a look of such devotion that you can't do anything but smile.

Boxers are eager to communicate. Many work out their own way of notifying their owners of what they want. For instance, looking at the refrigerator means he wants a treat; touching the back door with his paw means he wants to go out; when he brings his toy to you, you are supposed to throw it.

Boxers also love digging, particularly in the garden if he sees you doing it. Keep an eye on him, as he will carefully dig up each bulb you have planted.

The Reliable Nanny

Boxers simply love children, a quality that Boxer owners cherish. Perhaps it's because Boxers are childlike themselves that they recognize that quality in others.

Boxers know how to manipulate people much in the same way some children do, using their cuteness and neediness to implore adults for one more treat or one more game of tug.

Breed Truths

Boxers are generally a quiet breed, acting as a silent guardian in the home. When he barks, it's best to investigate, as he is not one to bark without cause.

The Intelligent Student

Boxers are one of the most intelligent breeds. If you don't watch out, they will outsmart you. You need to be the stronger partner, the one who sets the rules. While it's great to be the soul mate of a Boxer, your Boxer needs you to be his leader and guide.

You don't gain that position through yelling or force. Instead, you must earn his respect. Boxers have a sense of justice; they want to be treated fairly. He will accept your correction for chewing the chair leg or sneaking a bite of the baby's dinner. He knows he's wrong. But he'll be terribly hurt if he's blamed for something he didn't do, or if your anger is misplaced. Talk back to your boss, face up to your foes, and be pushy in offering your new ideas at work—just *don't* take out any disappointments or frustrations on your Boxer. He knows he does not deserve that, and any misdirected wrath will break his heart.

When giving your Boxer commands, be serious, firm, and insistent, while keeping your sense of humor. His own sense of humor is the breed's great attraction. Don't extinguish it. Allow room for that free spirit to soar.

The Gifted Athlete

Strong and athletic, Boxers become unsettled unless they get exercise every day. Just like little kids, they struggle to pay attention when their muscles are jumping beneath their skin. To keep your Boxer healthy, you have to

exercise with him. Fortunately, this is good for you, too. Two long walks a day, morning and night, are definitely what the doctor ordered for both of you.

If you can't walk him, you'll need a tennis ball or Frisbee to throw for him, to burn up some of his considerable energy. The same regimen is recommended for all energetic dogs, whether Labrador Retrievers or Jack Russell Terriers. If your Boxer is not exercised, he may take his energy out on something else, like your favorite chair, your shoes, or the piano leg.

He will make a great jogging partner and will always be up for a hike. He'll even agree to carry a backpack and lead the way. At the same time, at the end of the day, he will gladly sack out with you on the sofa.

Of course, the Boxer's primary goal in life is to be with his family. Keep him away and the chances are high that he'll dig up your flowerbeds or go crazy barking at squirrels. A bored Boxer knows how to get in trouble. He'll think up some way to entertain himself.

A crate is a great tool for a Boxer. When trained properly, a Boxer can learn to love his crate. Show him that it's his place to sleep comfortably, get a treat, and be undisturbed. (For more information on crates, see pages 61 to 62.)

Until you know that the only thing your Boxer will do while you're away is lie down and go to sleep, don't leave him loose in your house. You may think he's a sweet, innocent creature until you return home to find that he's chewed through the electrical cables, nibbled on the windowsills, and helped himself to the loaf of bread on the counter.

Breed Truths

Breeds Related to the Boxer

Old English Bulldog
Bernese Mountain Dog
Bullmastiff
Doberman Pinscher
Dogue de Bordeaux
Great Dane
Great Pyrenees
Greater Swiss Mountain Dog
Komondor
Kuvasz
Mastiff

The Loyal Protector

Boxers are natural guard dogs. They were selected for this quality more than one hundred years ago, as the breed was being established, and it remains one of the Boxer's innate characteristics. Most will look after family members, home, and property without any training. His strong appearance is certain to dissuade burglars who may think of breaking into a Boxer's home while he is on duty.

Even if he doesn't make a sound, the Boxer's tough appearance is enough to make burglars think twice about breaking into your house. A Chicago Boxer owner recalled how her Boxer seemed friendly and outgoing with everyone, until a man tried to open the windows when she was home alone. Then, he turned into a furious protector, growling and snapping until the intruder gave up and disappeared back into the night.

A Boxer quickly learns his family's routine and follows it. He knows the sound of the keys being picked up, which means you are about to leave. He will be waiting at the door because he knows the time you will return. If you go to bed every night at 10 P.M., you will soon find your Boxer urging you to the bedroom at 9:59. Some owners report that their Boxers know the difference between the suits they wear to the office and the jeans they wear to relax. When he sees the suit, he goes to his crate. When he sees the jeans, he gets his leash or a ball because it's playtime.

Boxers at Play

Puppies start boxing with their mother and littermates when they are about three weeks old. Since not every dog is a Boxer who understands the "paw slam," it's wise to teach Boxers to respond to a *no paw* command so they will greet other dogs without batting them immediately.

Boxers love a back rub and often wriggle on their backs on carpets, grass, or sand, trying to itch every spot. Gentle touch is also important to Boxers. They love to rub against your knees or lean on your shoulder, and often rub up against other dogs as well.

People purchasing a new puppy often ask, "Should I get a second dog, so he's not lonely?" If you are gone for long periods of time, getting a second dog is a good idea. A second Boxer will mean that both dogs get lots of exercise playing outside. But if your Boxer has the company of someone in the family or another animal for most of the day, he won't be lonely.

Playdates with other dogs are a good way to give your dog the company of his own kind. Dogs love the chance to play with their other dogs. If your dog was raised by a caring breeder who weaned him from his dam at around five or six weeks of age, he will have learned from her to respect older, bigger dogs and not challenge them. All puppies try biting and challenging their mom, and she is quick to discipline them sharply. Canine moms are a lot stricter about enforcing good behavior than most owners.

A caring breeder makes sure the puppies stay with their siblings until about eight weeks of age. During that time, the puppies learn how to get along with other dogs. They learn that if you bite another puppy, he bites you back, which hurts, and then he won't play with you anymore, which is no fun. In this way, they learn to inhibit their own behavior.

Dogs from shelters and rescues have to be watched more carefully, as no one knows how they were raised. If they didn't have early experience with dog play as puppies, it is sometimes hard for them to know how to limit their aggression and tone down the roughhousing. Some rescues can learn these lessons and be trusted around other animals. Others need lots of guidance and supervision. Some dogs can never be trusted not to snap and bite around another dog.

During a playdate, safety is the responsibility of the owners. You should be able to read your own Boxer well enough to know if he is threatening another dog or feels threatened by one.

In terms of exercise, the benefit of a playdate is tremendous. If they have a big fenced area to run in, most dogs will immediately entertain themselves by running and chasing. More hesitant dogs may need balls or sticks thrown for them as encouragement to join in.

Fun Facts

In a recent survey*, 62 percent of dog owners said their canines were more dependable than their human friends.

40 percent said their dogs are more likely to notice that they've had a bad day.

72 percent would rather take a walk with their dog than with other humans.

33 percent said that when they are out of town, they miss their dogs more than they miss their significant others.

*from Wags Not Words survey by Pup-Peroni

Being with his own species is fulfilling to a dog in a way that being with humans can never be. Although Boxers love their human companions and usually prefer them to other dogs, playdates let them be carefree canines for a while.

Boxers and Other Pets

Boxers desire human companionship over that of any of their fellow crea-
tures. While some Boxers tolerate other dogs or cats in the house, others are
jealous and don't like other animals near their owners.

That said, the breed seems to have a natural affinity for cats. They even
use their paws like cats, often batting at toys and touching people. An online
search will turn up many funny videos of Boxers and cats rolling around on
the floor in play.

The Healing Power of Boxers

Researchers have discovered many ways in which dog-human interactions
are healing. When you see your Boxer, your blood pressure decreases
and your heart rate slows. Your brain releases the hormone oxytocin—
sometimes called nature's "feel-good" hormone—into your bloodstream,
which produces a nurturing feeling.

When you pet your Boxer, your muscles initiate a relaxation response.
The theory behind the therapy dog movement is that when your dog visits
a hospital or nursing home, he does these same things for strangers.
As long as they like dogs, patients often experience a tremendous boost
from a therapy dog visit.

COMPATIBILITY Is a Boxer the Best Breed for You?

ENERGY LEVEL	● ● ● ●
EXERCISE REQUIREMENTS	● ● ● ●
PLAYFULNESS	● ● ● ●
AFFECTION LEVEL	● ● ● ●
FRIENDLINESS TOWARD OTHER PETS	● ● ●
FRIENDLINESS TOWARD STRANGERS	● ●
FRIENDLINESS TOWARD CHILDREN	● ● ● ●
EASE OF TRAINING	● ● ●
GROOMING REQUIREMENTS	●
SHEDDING	●
SPACE REQUIREMENTS	● ● ●
OK FOR BEGINNERS	● ● ●

4 Dots = Highest rating on scale

Boxers seem to know when their owners are in pain. They are sensitive dogs who read your body language for signs of how you feel. In her memoir, the movie star Lauren Bacall described how her husband, Humphrey Bogart, had a very strong bond with their Boxers. While Bogie was dying, Harvey the Boxer lay by his side as if he understood what was happening, staying close, comforting, and supporting, but not getting in the way.

Breed Needs

Boxers Are Affectionate

Boxers like to show their affection by reaching out a paw to touch their humans, even when they are sleeping. As one owner says of his dog, "He has to have some part of him touching me, even if it's only a toe or toenail. He wants me to always know that he is there."

In another story of Boxer sensitivity, a young woman noticed her Boxer paying particular attention when her elderly grandmother came for a visit. That night, she woke to barking and went out into the hall to see what was going on. She saw that her grandmother was trying to get to the stairs, but her Boxer refused to let her pass, bumping her legs and pushing her back. What she didn't know was that her grandmother had developed a seizure disorder that sometimes caused her to walk in her sleep. But the Boxer knew. He would not allow grandmom near the stairs, where she could be injured by a fall.

10 Questions About Boxers

1 What are the most important things to consider when choosing a Boxer? A boxer is a big dog who needs lots of exercise. He expects to be part of your life. He will be devoted to you and guard you from danger. As an added bonus, he needs very little grooming.

2 Will a Boxer be friendly to my children? Boxers are one of the most kid-friendly breeds. They seem to care instinctively about children and guard them protectively. They don't mind the swats and pinches that sometimes come from being friends with a youngster.

3 Will a Boxer take up a lot of my time? Yes. He will need at least two walks a day and he will expect to be a big part of your life. He can't be tied out in the backyard or left to roam the garden. More than anything else, a Boxer wants a person or a family to spend time with.

4 Do Boxers get along with cats? Generally, yes. It's always important to introduce Boxers to cats very carefully, keeping the Boxer on a leash so he can sniff the cat but not chase it. Of course, a lot will depend on the cat's attitude.

5 Do Boxers take to training? If you use positive methods and encourage him with treats and praise, a Boxer will easily take to training. They are smart dogs who often figure out on their own how to communicate their needs to their owners.

6 How can I get help training my Boxer? Start with a puppy training class at your local pet store. You can also join Boxer e-mail lists and discussion groups online, where experienced owners and breeders can answer your questions.

7 Can a Boxer make therapy dog visits to hospitals and nursing homes? Boxers do very well as therapy dogs. They seem to have a natural affinity for helping sick people and autistic children.

8 Can a Boxer compete in agility and flyball competitions? Boxers are excellent competitors if they think something's fun. With positive methods and rewards, they learn quickly. But because they are independent thinkers, they may sometimes veer off the course if something else catches their attention.

9 **What will I do with my Boxer when I go on vacation?** First, consider taking your Boxer with you. Many hotels and resorts now accept pets. Next, see if neighbors or friends might take him in, in return for being able to leave their pet with you when they go away. You can also investigate boarding kennels. Be sure to find a reputable one where he'll get outdoor exercise and good care.

10 **Is a Boxer good for my health?** Yes. Studies show that dog owners as a whole are healthier than the general population. They exercise more and make fewer visits to the doctor for minor illnesses. Plus, Boxers are good nurses. They like to comfort and support you whenever you don't feel well, for whatever reason.

Chapter Three

How to Choose
a Boxer

After much consideration, you've decided that a Boxer is the perfect pet for your family. Now you have to find the puppy or adult who will be a good match. Because Boxers are popular, there are many dogs to choose from. How do you find the right one?

Basically, you choose your new puppy first with your head and then with your heart. You have to figure out whether the new family member should be young or adult, male or female, fawn or brindle or white, a show prospect, or an abandoned shelter dog. When you're in the presence of puppies or mature dogs who fit the bill, let your heart take over to decide which one will be your companion for the next decade. It's an important decision.

Also, you want to leave part of the decision up to the puppy. Boxers have an uncanny ability to sense which human is their perfect match. Sit down with your prospective canine and talk it over with him. If your heart is speaking, he'll hear you.

What to Look For in Your New Family Member

The science of genetics tells us that a puppy will grow up to look and act a lot like his parents. In addition to carrying her genes, a puppy will pick up cues about how to behave from his mother during his first weeks of life. Breeders say a father and son may share personality traits as well.

If there's an opportunity, it's a great idea to meet the puppies' mother. At show kennels, the mother (also called the dam) is usually present. The father (also called the sire) might not be on the grounds because show breeders often travel great distances to breed their females to the healthiest and most handsome male, even if he belongs to another breeder. The breeder will know a lot about both parents and be able to answer all of your questions about health and temperament. He or she will also have photos of ancestors in the puppies' family tree.

Only a small number of buyers will be able to get a puppy from a show kennel, however. Show breeders simply don't produce enough puppies to meet the demand. But there are breeders who focus on producing healthy,

FYI: Singles and Boxers

Although experts tend to emphasize Boxers' bond with children, Boxers also do just fine in households of single men or women. Once you have picked a Boxer and he's picked you, he's yours for life. Your job in the relationship is to be the parent, the one dispensing love and discipline and setting the rules. The Boxer's job is to love you, entertain you, and protect you.

happy Boxers as pets, even if they won't be dog show competitors. Pet breeders might put ads in the newspaper, pet store, veterinarian's office, or online. At their homes, you may be able to meet both parents. Again, if the sire isn't present, ask about him. A good breeder should know all about the dog who sired the litter.

It is not enough to know that the puppy is registered; you want to know which registry was used. All dog registries are not equal. The American Kennel Club is strict about DNA typing, correct paperwork, and inspections of kennels. Other registries may be concerned only with a document stating breed and ownership.

When buying a puppy, be sure to evaluate the following:

1. **General attitude.** Boxer puppies typically play hard with their littermates and run to greet new friends. An active, alert, happy puppy is probably in good health. A listless puppy who won't come out of his bed to play with the others may be sick. If he's the one you prefer, come back on another day to see if he acts differently.
2. **Soundness.** Watch the puppy at play to make sure he doesn't limp or favor one leg. Watch him trotting across the floor. Notice if he constantly shakes or stretches, which might indicate a potential problem.
3. **Breathing.** Hold him and look directly in his face. The nostrils should be well opened for easy breathing. Checking a Boxer puppy's nostrils is important because some puppies are born with narrow or shut nostrils (stenotic nares) that can compromise their normal breathing. Because of their brachycephalic muzzles, Boxers sometimes emit a lot of breathing sounds. This may be normal. But a puppy with a cough needs a visit to the veterinarian, where he may get antibiotics. He should be isolated from other dogs until he recovers, as kennel cough is very contagious to other dogs (although not to humans).
4. **Stool.** You don't always get a chance to see a puppy's stool, but if he does eliminate, the stool should be firm and well formed. A loose stool could be a sign of worms or intestinal infection. These are common puppy conditions and not serious, but they should be treated before he goes to a new home.

5. **Skin.** Boxer skin is smooth and soft to the touch. If the puppy scratches, pick him up and check that spot. Red spots or dry patches could be anything from fleas to a skin allergy to ringworm.
6. **Eyes.** His eyes should be open and clear, without discharge.
7. **Body.** His body should be warm, but not hot to the touch. If he does feel hot, the breeder or kennel owner may need to take his temperature. It should be between 100 and 101.5°F.

Importance of the Pedigree

All puppies are beautiful. But before you fall in love with one of them, you want to make sure he will grow up to be as healthy as possible. For another clue to his family's health, ask the breeder to see the pedigree. This gives the names of the puppy's sire and dam and all his ancestors. Show breeders are proud to have dogs who are champions (indicated by "Ch." before the name) listed in the pedigree. A show champion has to be sound, fit, healthy, and good-tempered in order to win the title, so having champions in the pedigree is a good sign.

Another thing you might want to look for is any names that occur in the pedigree twice or more. For instance, if the sire and dam have exactly the same names behind them, they are brother and sister. If the dam's name is in the sire's pedigree, she is his mother or grandmother. There is an ongoing debate about whether such breeding may lead to bad health. Geneticists believe that most inherited illnesses are recessive traits. A dog could have a dominant gene for a strong heart and be healthy, yet carry a recessive gene

for heart disease. If two of his children are bred together (a brother-sister breeding), the resulting puppies could come up with heart disease.

In England, the Kennel Club has announced that it will no longer register the puppies of brother-sister, father-daughter, and son-mother breedings. The KC hopes to encourage breeders to create healthier dogs by using a more diverse gene pool.

When looking for a Boxer, it's important to ask about the health of the family line. Have any family members been affected by allergies? Is there any tendency to bloat in the family line? (Bloat, or gastric dilation, is discussed more fully in the chapter on Boxer health. See page 102.) Boxers are among the breeds known to be prone to heart disease. Has the breeder had the parents checked?

FYI: The Importance of Registries

The prestigious registries that have been around for one hundred years or more are the American Kennel Club (AKC) and United Kennel Club (UKC) in the United States, the Canadian Kennel Club (CKC) in Canada, and the Kennel Club (KC) in England. Registries can't tell you if a dog is healthy or sound in temperament, but they can provide other valuable information. They keep records of ownership and track which dogs have earned championships. They require breeders to send in DNA verification of their breeding stock for frequently used sires. Inspectors visit kennels and check the living conditions and accuracy of paperwork.

Because the rules of the AKC, UKC, CKC, and KC are so strict and demanding, and because fees are high, rival registries have sprung up in recent years. There are now about thirty registries in the United States, including America's Pet Registry (APR), American Canine Association (ACA), Dog Registry of America (DRA), and American Purebred Registry (APR). At present, none of them require DNA verification of pedigrees. While their paperwork might look similar, dogs in these registries generally cannot compete in the thousands of dog shows, field trials, agility competitions, and other events sponsored by the AKC and other big organizations.

When you ask the breeder about registration, make sure you get a clear answer as to which registry was used. It does make a difference.

What about hip dysplasia—have the parents been x-rayed? Hip dysplasia can be passed from parent to puppy. It is a disease of the hip joint that interferes with the dog's movement, and a bad case can cause the Boxer a lot of pain. As it is easily confirmed through X-rays, Boxer breeders should have the parents' hips x-rayed and rated. The Orthopedic Foundation for Animals (OFA) assigns a rating of fair, good, or excellent, which goes directly onto the AKC registration papers—another reason to insist on an AKC-registered puppy. At this time, none of the other registries put the hip rating on the papers. (There is a more complete discussion of hip dysplasia on page 104 in the chapter on Boxer health.)

A good breeder will talk to you honestly about health problems in the line. Don't be discouraged if the breeder tells you openly about any tendency to illness. There are potential health problems in every line and in every canine on earth. If all Boxers had perfect health, they would all live to be a hundred years old. But as we know, that doesn't happen. A life span of 10 to 13 years is about average. Ask the breeder if you can keep in touch so that, even when the dog is older, you have someone to contact for advice. Not every veterinarian has owned or raised a Boxer, but an experienced breeder will have advice that may be very useful to you.

You'll need a veterinarian to verify the health of your new puppy. He or she will check the puppy's temperature and make sure he's normally active

FYI: Cropped or Natural Ears?

If uncropped, Boxer ears frame the dog's face. They are of moderate size, thin, and lie flat along the cheek when at rest. When alert, the ear is raised slightly at the base and the leather falls forward.

In the show ring, most Boxers have their ears cropped to an erect triangle. The breed standard does not require the ears to be cropped; it says only that they are "customarily cropped." In the United States, the decision whether or not to crop rests with the breeder or owner.

Boxers once worked as sentries and guards, relying primarily on their keen hearing to do the job. Originally, owners cropped their Boxers' ears because they believed their dogs could hear better that way. However, experiments have shown that is not true. Dogs hear just as well whether their ears are cropped or not.

Another, even earlier reason to crop the ears was to eliminate soft folds of skin, which could be grabbed by the bull's teeth during bullbaiting. The same rationale applied to hunting; hunters did not want their dogs to be grabbed and pulled by their ears when subduing a bear or wild boar during the hunt.

Today, cropping is done only for cosmetic purposes. It requires surgery by a veterinarian. Show exhibitors in the United States tend to prefer the cropped ears because they look alert and active. Cropped ears can be beautifully shaped, while natural ears are larger and bulkier. Show judges often lean toward the dogs with cropped ears because the picture they present is sharp and neat.

Cropping has been banned in England, all European countries, and Australia, as well as banned in some states. There is a growing trend among show breeders in the United States and Canada to leave Boxer ears natural.

and not limp or lethargic. The doctor will also check for hernias, which occur if the hole where the umbilical cord was attached doesn't close all the way. Most umbilical hernias are small and not serious. The other type of hernia is inguinal, which produces a slight swelling on either side of the abdomen.

The veterinarian will examine the body for fleas, ticks, and skin irritations. He or she will gently manipulate the legs, making sure the patellas (kneecaps) are in place and there are no obvious hip deformities. On the skull, he or she will check to see if there is a soft spot where the bone of the skull does not fully cover the brain. The veterinarian will check the puppy's face to make sure his nostrils are open and the eyes are clear, not red or inflamed, and then check the mouth for healthy pink gums and normal baby teeth.

The veterinarian will use an otoscope to probe the ear canal and a stethoscope to listen to the heart, checking for any arrhythmia. Finally, a stool sample is checked for worms.

How to Find a Puppy

To find Boxer puppies, ask friends who own Boxers where they got theirs. Ask people in dog parks walking Boxers. Attend dog shows, where Boxer exhibitors may be able to give you some advice. You may meet your next best friend in a pet shop.

The Internet

Another strategy is to make use of the new world of social media right in your home. There are an amazing number of websites devoted to Boxers. Through the Internet, you can research Boxers to your heart's content. One of the first places to turn is YouTube or another video site. A search for "Boxer dogs" will bring up dozens of videos, most of them posted by proud owners of handsome and sometimes funny Boxers. Some breeders also post videos to show off their puppies.

You can also find e-mail lists of people who own Boxers and like to discuss them. These can be a good resource for finding a Boxer breeder. For example, on Yahoo Groups, you will find *boxerlovers@yahoogroups.com*, *white-boxer@yahoogroups.com*, *bxf@yahoogroups.com*, *agileboxers@yahoogroups.com*,

Helpful Hints

The American Boxer Club recommends that breeders have their dogs tested before breeding for hip and elbow dysplasia, hypothyroidism, aortic valve disease, aortic stenosis, and cardiomyopathy. Ask the breeder if those tests have been done.

CHECKLIST

Questions a Breeder Might Ask You

- ✔ Have you ever had a Boxer before?
- ✔ Why do you want one?
- ✔ Have you cared for a dog before?
- ✔ What happened to your last dog?
- ✔ What will the puppy's life be like with you?
- ✔ If you are away from home more than eight hours a day, will some-

one else be available to care for him?

- ✔ Is this puppy planned as a surprise present? (Most breeders will not allow this, because they want to know that the dog is truly wanted and that the new owner is prepared to take on the responsibility of training and caring for him.)

Dancing_With_Boxers@yahoogroups.com, and others. Many other sites, including Google, AOL, MSN, and Meetup, host groups for Boxer people. The number of online chat rooms for Boxers increases every month.

The AKC website offers a lot of information for potential Boxer owners. Classified ads for available puppies are listed by breed and state. The AKC also provides phone numbers for 25 Boxer rescue groups located across the country. The AKC encourages buyers to work with a responsible breeder, and it suggests several resources for locating breeders:

- Contact the parent club, the American Boxer Club. You'll be connected to a volunteer club member who will give you a list of breeders in your area who may have puppies. On the weekends, these people are often away at dog shows, so if you don't get an answer, call again.
- Visit *americanboxerclub.org*, where you will find an extensive list of local Boxer clubs. Check to see if there is one near you. Each Boxer club's website gives more specific information about breeders in the area. There are currently 55 Boxer clubs in 33 states.
- If there is no local Boxer club, check the AKC website for an all-breed club in your city. Members may know who breeds Boxers locally.

You'll pull up an endless number of sites when you search "Boxer puppies" on the Web. This gives you many chances to find a Boxer breeder. But a buyer needs to be careful, because schemes abound. One potential Boxer owner, Matthew, corresponded with a faraway breeder, who sent him photos of puppies. Matthew chose an adorable six-month-old brindle female puppy. The breeder urged him to send money and she would ship the puppy, but Matthew wasn't comfortable with that. He wanted to see the puppy first before buying her. He flew from his home in Manhattan to the kennel in Missouri. When he got there, he was unpleasantly surprised. "She showed me a lot of puppies, but not the one in the photo," he said. "That

puppy didn't exist. They were planning to ship me a puppy who looked completely different." He left in disgust.

Not everyone can afford to fly to another state to pick up a dog. Some unethical breeders count on that. They know that once they ship the puppy to you, chances are you will fall in love with him, even if he is not the one you were promised. When you discover the switch, they will claim that the original puppy was sick or injured at the last moment. If you sent money from another state, you have little recourse. Interstate lawsuits can only be initiated if the value is more than $5,000, which is unlikely in this case. Hiring a lawyer would be too expensive. Even if the puppy is registered,

CHECKLIST

Important Questions to Ask the Breeder

- ✔ How old are the pups?
- ✔ Which sex is available?
- ✔ Have they had their shots and worming?
- ✔ Did they get a health check from a veterinarian?
- ✔ Is the litter AKC-registered?
- ✔ Were the pups handled frequently? Are they well-socialized?

- ✔ What kind of food are they eating?
- ✔ Are the parents, littermates, or any family members available, so I can get an idea of what the puppies will be like when they're grown?
- ✔ Will I have 72 hours to take the puppy to a veterinarian? If he's sick, is there a money-back guarantee? (Many states have "puppy lemon laws" that require this.)

the registry wouldn't be able to help you, as it doesn't have authority in a sales dispute.

To avoid such scenarios, it's best to buy your puppy locally if you can.

Newspaper Ads

Here is a typical ad posted by a Boxer breeder:

"Available: flashy brindle male, $700; one black female and one fawn male, $600. Tails and dewclaws; first shots and deworming. Pups are socialized, friendly, and ready to go on June 1. Sire and dam are here for you to meet. Photos are available upon request."

Let's decode this ad. By "flashy brindle," the breeder means a puppy who is brindle with lots of white markings. He will likely have a white muzzle, white collar and breast, and white legs. The fact that this puppy costs more than the others probably means that he is a show prospect.

"One black female" may be misleading to newcomers to the Boxer world. The Boxer puppy is not really black; she is brindle, which means fawn with lots of black tiger stripes. She does not have flashy white markings like the first puppy. "Fawn male" means a Boxer puppy in the classic shiny shade, which varies from light tan to mahogany. This puppy also does not have flashy white markings. The Boxer standard insists that plain colors are equal to flashy markings. But experienced exhibitors know that the flashy markings give a Boxer an advantage with many judges.

By "Tails and dewclaws," the breeder means that the puppies' tails have been docked in the classic Boxer fashion, which is usually done at three to five days old. It causes the puppy no more than a moment of discomfort. In England and Europe, tails are no longer docked, so they are long and thick. The dewclaw is an undeveloped toe on the inside of the dog's front leg, inches above the foot. Evolutionists say it is a remnant from the time when canines' feet were substantially longer. Since the dewclaw

CAUTION

What if my child is allergic?

Boxers are among those breeds classified as hypoallergenic, meaning that they have a relatively low capacity to induce allergic reactions. There is no such thing as a totally non-allergenic breed. All dogs shed. Boxers shed less because they have a short, single coat. Boxers also have a low level of dander, particularly compared with many longhaired breeds. But the only way to know for sure if your child is allergic is through trial and error. Try visiting someone who owns a Boxer and note whether or not the dog induces allergic reactions in your child.

A recent medical study showed that children who grew up in homes with pets were less likely to develop allergies to animals. Children who were never exposed to pets were more likely to have reactions to them. When there was a pet in the house, the child's immune system learned how to handle the potential stressors of pet hair and dander.

can catch and injure the dog, it is usually removed at the same time as tail docking.

"First shots and deworming" are the normal medical procedures done on young puppies. From birth, they are protected from illness by the mother's immunity. This starts to wear off around 6 to 12 weeks, so a booster shot is given to tune up the immunity. The immature puppy's system can't hold onto the immunity, so a second shot is given three to four weeks later, and a third shot three to four weeks after that, when the puppy is around 16 weeks old.

"Socialized, friendly, and ready to go on June 1" is another good sign. Socializing puppies is one of the breeder's most important duties. Puppies should be raised in close proximity with humans, so that they are often touched, held, and spoken to in their first weeks. The more stimulation they receive as

If you are getting a Boxer primarily for your children, make sure the dog is one that you love as well. No matter how mature or how sincere, children need constant supervision and help to handle the responsibility of owning a dog. Ultimately, a parent is responsible for the feeding, walking, and training.

CHECKLIST

Puppy Paperwork

The breeder should supply you with:

✔ A record of the puppy's shots

✔ A health certificate from a veterinarian

✔ A registration application

✔ A pedigree

whelps, the more stable their temperaments will be as adults. Puppies usually leave home at about eight weeks. The AKC classified ad shows that this litter was born April 6, so June 1 will be their eight-week birthday.

The good thing about buying from a reputable breeder, as this is that one seems to be, you probably will be able to keep in touch with her as your puppy grows. Questions may come up that a breeder can answer in a quick phone call, instead of an expensive visit to the veterinarian's office.

Pet Stores

Many people obtain Boxers by buying them at the pet store. A pet store is one of the few places where a member of the public can easily see a little Boxer puppy. With their big eyes and quizzical expressions, Boxer puppies are irresistible. Even though the store may have an excellent reputation, try not to plunk down your money without finding out many of the same things you would find out from a breeder. Ask about the parents, where the puppy was born, and how he was raised. Is he registered? Has he had a veterinary check? Pet stores realize that people want to know these things, and many have the information on hand. Ideally, pet store clerks will know the breeder and be able to answer questions.

Helpful Hints

How to Get Out of the Kennel Without Buying a Puppy

If you don't think you've found the right puppy for you, don't buy one! It's normal for potential buyers to visit a kennel and then say they need to think over the decision a little more. If you see a problem, tell the breeder your reason directly—for example, that the puppy has runny eyes or loose stool, or you're concerned that the dam growled at your children.

What doesn't feel right to you probably isn't. Doubts you have now may grow into unhappiness with your pet purchase. Too often, that's when people turn their dogs over to shelters. It's best for both you and your new companion to make sure you are getting the Boxer you really want from the start.

BE PREPARED! What to Expect from a Boxer

- strong
- enthusiastic
- boisterous
- needs exercise
- attentive to children
- guards the house
- independent thinker
- sometimes stubborn
- easy to housetrain
- sense of humor

- sometimes naughty
- insists on being with family
- can't be left outside alone
- sensitive to heat and cold weather
- sometimes drools
- often snores
- prefers to be the only dog in the family
- resents sharing space, attention, toys, and treats with other dogs

Rescue and Shelter Adoption

Because the breed is so popular, many Boxers end up in rescue programs and shelters and need new homes. It's wonderful to be able to offer a second chance to a Boxer who has been rejected by his first owners. But it is not appropriate for everyone.

There are several ways to obtain an unwanted Boxer: from shelters, animal welfare organizations, and breed rescue. The adoption experience can be vastly different with each organization.

Shelters

Animals who are lost or unwanted by their owners are dropped off at shelters, where they are housed temporarily. The public can meet the dogs to see if they have potential as a family pet. Occasionally, Boxers may turn up at shelters. If you are looking for a Boxer, most shelters will take your name in case one arrives, but it's best to keep checking as it is easy for overworked personnel to forget to call you.

Breed Truths

Words owners use to describe their Boxers, young or old:

- Alert
- Friendly
- Fearless
- Loving
- Energetic
- Smart
- Brave
- Family-oriented
- Dignified
- Rowdy
- Funny
- Comical
- Silly
- Boisterous
- Devoted

According to shelters around the country, about 80 percent of the dogs are Pit Bulls. Sadly, Boxers are sometimes mistaken for Pit Bulls. When you are told that a certain shelter has a Boxer, be sure that it really is one, as a Pit Bull's personality is quite different. The Boxer's impish sense of humor sets him apart from other breeds.

Only about half the dogs in shelters are either returned to their original owners or find a new home. The rest are euthanized. But don't let this sad fact influence your decision and persuade you to take whatever dog you find. You are looking for a family friend and protector. You need to know that the dog you obtain will be able to trust you and form a loving bond. Some dogs are damaged by bad breeders or their first owners, making them unable to do so.

CAUTION

Adopt a Rescue Boxer If . . .

- He will not have to be around small children until you are sure he can be trusted not to react inappropriately (perhaps bite).
- Everyone in the family understands this is a "special needs" dog.
- You have patience with any strange habits he may have picked up from previous owners, including eliminating in the house.
- You have time to train him thoroughly in order to rehabilitate his behavior.

There are approximately 5,000 animal shelters in the United States. County and city shelters take in all stray animals and are paid with tax dollars. Volunteers usually run the private, nonprofit shelters. The American Society for the Prevention of Cruelty to Animals (ASPCA) maintains a database of shelters throughout the country that is accessible on its website, *ASPCA.org.*

Of the approximately three million dogs who end up in shelters every year, about one-quarter are purebred. Of those, a small percentage are Boxers. Almost none will be puppies. The dogs in shelters tend to be older dogs who were turned in because they are no longer as appealing as when they were younger. The number-one reason dogs are surrendered to shelters is housetraining problems. Boxers are usually easy to housetrain, but if untrained and neglected, they may pick up the habit of eliminating in the house.

A Boxer adopted from a shelter may pose special challenges. He may not have a good idea of how to behave in a family situation. It's best to be aware of such problems before you adopt. Shelter personnel do their best to evaluate each animal's behavior and spot possible problems. However, because unadopted dogs may face euthanasia, they are sometimes described in terms that make them seem family-friendly, even though they may not be. Be sure to visit with the dog and get a feel for his personality. Don't assume that the written description is 100 percent correct.

Adopting from a shelter usually costs between $100 and $300, which covers the cost of spaying or neutering the animal, as well as vaccinations and medical care.

FYI: What's In a Name

In the past, "strays" were rounded up by "dog catchers" and taken to the "pound." Today, the language has changed. "Homeless" dogs are found by "animal control" or "animal welfare" officers and taken to "shelters," where they are cared for until they can be "adopted." The new, gentler expressions reflect society's changing attitudes toward animal welfare.

Rescue Organizations

Not all lost or abandoned dogs end up in shelters. Some are taken in by private rescue organizations that arrange for temporary foster housing with volunteers. On the AKC website, there is a complete listing of Boxer rescue organizations throughout the United States. The American Boxer Rescue Association (ABRA) is comprised of many Boxer rescue organizations working together to help place Boxers in need, provide education, and promote responsible rescue efforts.

Through Internet searches, you may find other private rescue groups in your area. Many of these groups are made up of people doing their best to match the right dog with the right person. Some groups carry this to an extreme, asking the potential adopter to fill out 12-page applications and/or allow their homes to be inspected.

In any case, adopting a pet can be a bit like signing up for a dating service. You'll have to fill out an application, which includes your pet ownership history; details about your home, work, and family; and a personality profile. You will have to sign a contract promising to take good care of the Boxer and to return him to the shelter or rescue if you can no longer care for him. (Some shelters have a no-return policy, so make sure you know the details of your shelter before moving forward with an adoption.)

Rescue volunteers usually do their best to find out as much as possible about the Boxer as well. If they can, they ask the original owner whether he had any bad habits, like chewing shoes or furniture, urinating on the carpet, or biting. They check his health and screen for heartworm and other diseases. Some have animal behavior specialists evaluate the Boxer.

To find adoptable Boxers, a great place to start is *Petfinder.com*, a website devoted to connecting homeless animals with the people who want them. Petfinder works almost like an Internet dating service, allowing prospective adopters to search through photos of available pets, both close and far away. County and private animal groups, whether large or small, can display their inventory of dogs and cats. Petfinder lists 13,000 adoption groups and more than 323,000 adoptable pets—perhaps one who is perfect for you.

But even with *Petfinder.com*, you have to be careful. Entering "Boxer" with the location "Princeton, NJ" turned up a page with 24 available dogs.

Of these, 12 were listed as Pit Bull/ Boxer mixes, but 8 of those looked more like purebred Pit Bulls, showing none of the facial characteristics of Boxers. Only 7 of the 24 dogs on the page were listed as purebred Boxers, but a close reading of the ads revealed that 4 of those were not actually Boxers but mixes (the result of crosses with a German Shepherd, a Great Dane, a Mastiff, and a Labrador). "Porter is a boxer mix but has the full boxer personality, and a tail to boot!" one ad read.

Only 3 of the 24 dogs who came up in the search really were purebred Boxers. One had vision problems. His photo was not posted, possibly because his eyes were damaged and needed surgery.

The second Boxer, Reggie, was undoubtedly a purebred, although he was not in Princeton, NJ, the search area, but hours away in New York.

Fun Facts

The New Shelter

In former times, the animal shelter was usually a concrete building filled with long rows of metal cages, the smell of urine, and continuous barking. Some are still like that. But some, like Maddie's Pet Adoption Center in the San Francisco area, or Best Friends in Kanab, Utah, look more like five-star hotels. Millions of dollars in donations from generous dog lovers have enabled them to provide luxurious housing for their "guests." Dogs lounge on sofas, play with squeaky toys, and run in grassy paddocks. Volunteers work on socializing and training the dogs.

The ad looked like this:

"Points to Remember/Qualifying Criteria:

- A fenced yard is required—invisible fencing is not acceptable.
- Veterinary references are required.
- A home visit is required, no exceptions.
- No children under 7 years of age.
- There is a nonrefundable $250 adoption donation required. Note: We may request a higher adoption donation if an animal required extensive medical care. You will also be asked to complete an adoption contract at the time of adoption.
- Please understand that we will not discuss our animals with individual adopters until after the application process is completed.

The attached application was seven pages long and noted, "Visits with available animals are by appointment only once preapproved (thank you for your understanding)."

According to the ad, the Boxer, Reggie, had gone through several homes, could not tolerate cats, and was "exuberant with his toys, but responds well if you show him who is the pack leader." The rescuer continued, "This boy has lots of energy that was not properly addressed in his former homes and would greatly benefit from an experienced handler, preferably with Boxer experience."

It would be reasonable to conclude that this Boxer has personality quirks that would be a challenge for the average pet owner to handle. He may need more supervision, exercise, and training than a puppy. Before you adopt

CHECKLIST

A Reputable Rescue Group

The American Boxer Rescue Association publishes a list of the characteristics of a reputable rescue group:

✔ Screens applicants rigorously in order to find the most suitable home for each dog

✔ Completes a veterinary protocol before placement, to include spay/neuter

✔ Performs a home visit to ensure that each dog is going to a safe, stable home

✔ Willingly takes the dog back if the placement does not work out

✔ Temperament tests each dog to make sure the dog is sound

a Boxer like this one, make sure your family understands that extra time and training will be needed, and possibly the help of a professional dog trainer or canine behaviorist.

It has almost become fashionable to obtain your new dog from a shelter or animal welfare organization. Everyone admires someone who proclaims, "I rescued him." Many organizations are obsessed with the admiration they receive. Some make it almost impossible for a normal person to adopt a dog by inventing pages of rules and regulations for prospective adopters. Some breeders have joined the game by calling their puppies "rescues" and charging anywhere from $300 to $800 for them.

Another problem shelters face are the mentally ill people known as "animal collectors" or "hoarders." These individuals believe they are "rescuing" the many dogs who pile up in their homes. Eventually the responsibility overwhelms them, they stop taking care of the animals, and animal control officers and mental health professionals have to step in.

People don't turn in sweet, perfectly trained, obedient Boxers. They abandon the dog because he is a problem, even though it is most likely a problem they created. The Boxer is there because no one knew how to housetrain him, or he scared the kids, or he ran away because he was starved for exercise and affection, or possibly because he bit someone in response to a frightening situation.

It's wonderful to take a damaged dog and give him a new life. Just remember that it is not always possible for a dog to overcome the behavior problems he picked up in a bad situation. Before you decide to adopt an abandoned or abused dog, think carefully about your situation. Will your children be safe around a dog whose history is unknown? Will you be able to devote extra time to rehabilitating and retraining a scared or reactive dog? Sometimes, ads placed by rescues and shelters require reading between the lines.

FYI: Kennels

The word *kennel* does not necessarily mean a separate building with many fenced runs. Show breeders and pet breeders may keep only a few dogs who live in the house as family pets. Whether or not a breeder has a big building does not affect the quality of the puppies. These small breeders are able to raise their puppies in the home, where they get used to noise, commotion, and rowdy children, which is an advantage for the puppies.

Some Boxers may find their way into your home by other routes. One owner's two Boxers had a fight and thereafter couldn't get along. He was forced to give one of them to a friend, much to the friend's delight. His new Boxer girl was housetrained, leashtrained, and well behaved—she just didn't like her old housemate. As long as the two were apart, everything was fine.

Adult or Puppy?

When you acquire a puppy, you have a wiggling bundle of potential. You will have to train him and shape his behavior constantly. An older Boxer will be more settled and less exuberant. It's easier to train an older Boxer because he will have a longer attention span than a puppy.

Show kennels often release their older Boxers to pet homes once they are finished with their show ring career. These dogs are accustomed to behaving well in spite of multiple distractions and are comfortable being handled. They make terrific pets.

Some older Boxers surrendered to shelters or rescues will be equally stable, but it's best to inquire and learn as much as

CAUTION

Meet the Parents

Listen to your intuition when you meet the sire and dam of your prospect. Their behavior will tell you what the behavior of the puppy is likely to be. If they are aggressive, this trait will be passed on. If they are fearful, the puppy will have already learned this behavior.

Notice not only how the parents react to you, a stranger, but also how they interact with their owners. They might be standoffish about a stranger in the house at first, but they should quickly accept new people when the owners let them know it's okay.

possible about their background. Adopting an adult means you won't have to contend with puppy chewing. He may even be leashtrained and housetrained. There are many advantages to adopting an adult Boxer, in addition to giving him a second chance.

Male or Female?

Some people claim that male Boxers are calmer and more tolerant, while others claim that females are. Some think males are more loving, but other Boxer owners can point to incredibly loving females.

Whether you adopt a male or female Boxer is strictly a matter of personal preference. There are no clearly defined personality characteristics separating the sexes; their Boxer traits are the same. Females can be tough and males can be delicate. A female Boxer protecting her family may be formidable, and a male Boxer cuddling with the kids on the floor can be nurturing.

Some people want a female because they worry that a male may mark his territory. But a properly trained male Boxer respects the cleanliness of the home he lives in and waits to be taken outside. Owners of males report that the dogs hold their urine even if the owner is terribly late getting home.

Breed Truths

The Boxer-Human Bond

Raising your Boxer from an eight-week-old adorable puppy creates a wonderful bond between the two of you. But the surprising fact is you can form an equally strong bond if you adopt an older Boxer. You *can* teach an older Boxer new tricks. It might take a little longer to establish a training relationship, but that's okay. Work on it every day. An advantage is that an older Boxer has a longer attention span than a bouncy, young puppy. Your training sessions will be rewarding for both of you.

Some people want a male because they worry that a female will get pregnant. It's true that having a female in heat requires strict supervision to make sure she doesn't get loose and mate with a male dog. But when you take on ownership of the dog, you take on that responsibility. When females are fully mature, which means over one year old, they can be spayed. Twenty-five percent of spayed bitches develop "spay leaks," an inability to hold their urine because of damage to the muscles that hold the bladder closed. There are doggy diapers available for this problem.

As you can see, there is no correct answer to the "male or female?" question. Better to pick the puppy that most appeals to you.

Reasons to Adopt an Older Boxer

When elderly Boxers are put up for adoption, they are usually calmer and more reliable than puppies. They are not likely to be upset by household chaos, for example. But it's important to realize that the breed is not long lived, with 10 to 13 being the usual life span.

Elderly Boxers will certainly enhance the life of the person willing to adopt them. One woman who adopted an older Boxer wrote, "Tingle was five years old when I adopted her. Yes, I very much missed the puppy stage. But at my age, I did not miss housetraining, leashtraining, and all the other joys that go into raising a puppy. Sometimes an older dog is just what is needed."

White Boxers

Approximately 25 percent of all Boxer puppies born to parents that have white markings are either white or almost all white. White Boxers are therefore not rare or unusual but a common occurrence in the breed. Some white pups have brindle or fawn patches on the head, body, or base of the tail. These almost all-white puppies are sometimes referred to as "checks" or "parti-colors."

There have always been beautiful white Boxers in the breed. The all-white gene was introduced with crosses to a white English Bulldog in the 1890s. White Boxers were accepted for registration and breeding by the German Boxer Club up until 1925. They were banned because the club decided the Boxer was a specialist as a police and guard dog. White was not acceptable for that work because a white dog would be too visible to an enemy.

White Boxers can be AKC-registered, but they cannot be shown. None of the national parent clubs in any country permit the breeding of white Boxers, even though white Boxers are exactly the same in temperament and structure as their pigmented siblings. The reason for the breeding ban concerns their health. White dogs have a higher incidence of deafness than

dark-colored dogs in every breed, not only in Boxers but also in Dalmatians, Bulldogs, Bull Terriers, Pointers, Whippets, and others.

There are, however, devoted fans of white Boxers who do breed for the white color. These fans anecdotally report no higher incidence of deafness than in colored Boxers, but there has not yet been a published study to that effect. Until there is, the American Boxer Club asks its members not to register white Boxers and not to include white Boxers in the count on the AKC litter application form. By disallowing white, the ABC is trying to avoid future health problems.

Once you start your search for a Boxer, the right one may find his way to you— brindle or white, young or old. One happy owner got her Boxer through a twist of fate: "Angel is four years old now and the light of my life, but she is not the one I picked. When they were only three weeks old, I fell in love with a fawn female. I gave half the money as a deposit on that puppy. But when I came to pick her up, the breeder had given that puppy to her son. I was upset. I sat on the floor, and a tiny female came over and crawled into my lap. To this day, we are inseparable. I take her everywhere. The bond between us is so strong. Now that I'm doing rescue work, people always want to adopt her and I have to tell them that she's mine and not up for adoption. She is my soul mate. Not the puppy I wanted, but exactly the right puppy anyway."

Fun Facts

The International White Boxer Club, which is based in Germany, is working to restore white Boxers to the breed standard.

Chapter Four

Caring for a Boxer Puppy

Your new Boxer puppy comes to you with the potential to be a loving, trusted member of the family. From there, it is up to you to instruct him on how to behave in his new home. You need to be the kind leader who shows him what to do and corrects him when he does something wrong. You need to be calm, assertive, and consistent in your training.

You also need to view his training as an ongoing process that will build a bond between the two of you. The more you train, the more you will come to understand each other. Training is not something you do once a day in a quiet place. It is an everyday occurrence that takes place whenever the two of you are together: in the kitchen, out for a walk, or on the sofa watching television.

Everything that happens is an opportunity to teach him something. If you are not teaching him, he is teaching you. Here are some of the things your puppy wants to teach you:

- Give me a treat every time I look cute.
- Never tell me to get off the sofa.
- Let me go out any time I want.
- It's okay for me to jump on people when they come to the door.
- Don't correct me if I make mistakes in the house.
- It's okay if I don't come when you call.
- When a door opens, I can rush through.
- I can take any food I want.
- Shoes are delicious .
- I can bark all I want.

He will try to teach you these things every time the situation arises. Therefore, you must be clear about what you want him to do at all times. Make sure all family members agree on the rules. If you have decided never to let him on the couch, the kids must keep to that. If they let him on the couch now and then, it will be impossible to keep him off. He'll be confused by conflicting instructions.

When he picks up a shoe, he must be told *"Drop it."* Every time. Give him a toy instead. As he begins to chew the piano leg, tell him *"No."* Again, substitute a toy. When you call him, he must come. Don't let him slide now

and then. He has to do it every time, or he has just trained you that it is not necessary.

It's hard for humans to be consistent. Often, dogs are better trainers of humans than we are of them.

The First Week

The first week is a difficult time. Your puppy has to acclimate to many things in your home that he has not encountered before. No matter how well socialized he was by the breeder, the first week will be a time of transition, a time of trial and error. Decide ahead of time to remain calm and work through this period slowly and carefully.

Show him his food and water bowl, let him sniff his new bed, and sit with him and introduce his new toys. Puppies are most concerned with playing.

Take him outside and show him the area where he's to do his business. If you're lucky, he'll pee at the right spot, allowing you to praise him: *"Good boy! What a clever boy!"* Reward him with a treat.

Once he's had at least two sets of shots, you can take him shopping with you to pick out his collar (so you can make sure it fits). Pet stores allow dogs to accompany their owners as they shop. It's a good place to start his training and continued socialization. (You can also check on times of puppy classes while you're there.)

If you haven't been in a pet store lately, you'll be amazed at the number of products now being sold for dogs. There are vast rows of designer collars and leashes, biscuits and treats of infinite variety, and dog beds that are comfy and fashionable.

Puppy Necessities

Collar The best collar for a puppy is a nylon adjustable one, so that you can keep letting it out as he grows. Collars need to be tight enough so that they will not slip off over his head, even if something frightens him while you are out walking and he suddenly pulls away. You don't want him to be able to slip out of his collar and run into the street.

The fit is correct if you can slip your fingers under the collar, but not so loose that you can pull it off. You should take it off every two weeks to make it slightly larger.

Leather or rolled leather collars work equally well as nylon ones. Most trainers don't recommend choke chains anymore, as today's positive training methods are best accomplished with a regular collar.

Leashes You'll need two kinds of leashes: a short, six-foot leash and a flexible, retractable leash. Do not use a chain leash, which will be heavy on his neck and your hand. Other than that, Boxers do not care what kind of leash you buy—nylon, cotton, rope, or leather.

The retractable leash should be the medium or large size, which extend to 15 feet (6 m). It is easier to teach a Boxer to do his business outside if you walk him on the retractable leash. Boxers who have been raised properly don't want to relieve themselves close to you. They want to move a short distance away, sometimes even behind a bush or tree. The retractable lead

SHOPPING LIST

Puppy Supplies

Must-Haves:
- ✔ Collar
- ✔ Leash
- ✔ ID tag
- ✔ Water and food dishes
- ✔ Bed
- ✔ Kennel crate
- ✔ Brushes
- ✔ Nail clippers and Kwik Stop styptic powder
- ✔ Toys

- ✔ Tennis ball
- ✔ Bones, biscuits, and treats

Optional:
- ✔ Dog toothbrush and toothpaste
- ✔ Gauze
- ✔ Seatbelt attachment
- ✔ Exercise pen
- ✔ Dog litter box
- ✔ Sweaters or coats
- ✔ Halter lead

HOME BASICS
Introducing the Puppy to Other Pets

If you have other animals, take the time to introduce them to the new puppy. Hold each animal securely so they can't run and hide. Assure the older pet that the new puppy is welcome and does not represent any change in status or danger to him. Hold the puppy and let him sniff the air to get used to the other pet. Assure him that he will be welcome.

You don't want the cat or older dog to run away with the puppy chasing after him. That will set them off to a bad start. It's better to let them observe each other for a few minutes in the arms of family members before setting them loose together.

When the older pet and new puppy get together, the older pet will want to let the youngster know that he is the low guy in the pecking order. It's best to be patient and let the two canines work this out. It is normal if the older dog growls a little and gives the puppy a hard stare. The well-socialized puppy's response should be to lower his body, lie on his back, bow, or dip his head, all representing the equivalent of,

"I know you are in charge. I am not trying to defy you. Let's be friends."

If the two of them can work this out, there will be peace in your home. Don't interfere unless the older dog shows signs of biting or hurting the puppy, and the puppy squeals in fear. Then you have to step in and reprimand the older dog, reminding him, "I'm in charge here and both of you must listen to me."

Alternatively, if your puppy is young and rambunctious and your older dog is frail, don't let the youngster hurt him. Tell the puppy "*Settle!*" or "*Calm!*"

Older dogs are great puppy trainers. They demand obedience, sometimes ordering the puppy to lie down and stay there for extended periods, as much as 10 or 20 minutes. If this happens, leave them alone. The puppy is learning a valuable lesson in patience and obedience. Dogs are more persistent than humans. No human dog trainer would try to keep the puppy in a *down-stay* for such a long time. Dogs are very insistent on discipline. We should learn from them.

gives him room to do this. He'll relieve himself and come happily back without tripping or tangling the leash. Even a Boxer who has his own back-yard in which to relieve himself needs to be taught that he can go when on a leash, so that you'll be comfortable taking him with you on trips.

Identification tag The best identification for your dog is a tag with your phone number inscribed on it in large numbers. Studies have shown that a lost dog with a phone number on the collar is most likely to be returned. The finder's first impulse will be to call that number. Dogs without identification tags are more likely to be turned into a pound or shelter.

Buy a tag on which your phone number will be clearly displayed, and be sure to use your cell phone number. If he's lost, you are likely going to be out looking for him and can take your cell phone with you. If you want to add other information, it's best to put it on the other side, so the phone number is as big as possible. You might want to engrave his name, your name and address, or a second phone number on the other side.

Water and food dishes It's a good idea to put a mat down under his food and water bowl for two reasons: one, in case of spills, and two, because Boxers often drool water droplets after they drink. Some Boxers splash water with their paws, especially in hot weather when they are trying to cool off. If your Boxer loves water, buy him a shallow plastic baby swim-ming pool and put it in the backyard. He will quickly realize that splashing in water is amusing to humans and spend hours entertaining you.

Get two separate dishes, rather than the connected two-in-one dishes. Separate dishes make it easier to refill one when you don't need to refill the other.

Puppies need their dishes placed on the floor. Older dogs are comfortable if their bowls are slightly higher. You can make a platform 6 to 12 inches high with a box, or buy one from the pet store.

Bed A Boxer loves a comfortable bed. If you don't want him to sleep on your bed, he needs a crate or bed in your room. If you are using a crate, get a thick soft blanket or cushion to put in it. If you don't want him on the furniture, get a bed for the living room so that he has a place to relax while you are watching television in your easy chair. If you spend a lot of time on the computer, put a bed in your office or study. Boxers like to keep an eye on the people they own.

Donut beds are plush and soft, and the dog can curl up against the cushioned sides. Canvas or nylon beds are raised a few inches off the floor. You can get beds from the corner discount store or a fancy furniture shop.

CAUTION

Delicious Beds

Do not buy beds made of foam cushions for young puppies, as they tend to chew them apart and eat the foam. If they do, the foam usually comes out in the stool, but it could potentially cause a blockage. Foam beds are fine for older dogs, but while he's a puppy, use a blanket or bed without stuffing.

CHECKLIST

Optional Items

- ✔ Gauze: Gauze can be used as a toothbrush. Put it on your finger to rub his teeth.
- ✔ Seatbelt: A seatbelt is just as good an idea for a dog as it is for you. The belt is attached to a harness, not a collar, so you'll need to pick up a harness, too.
- ✔ Exercise pen: A metal exercise pen is used to keep him confined in a small area. It can be used as a temporary gate to block him from going into the kitchen or other room.
- ✔ Dog litter box: The same as a cat litter box, the dog litter box is a relatively new idea in housetraining. It's good for dogs who live in apartments.
- ✔ Coats and sweaters: Since Boxers are sensitive to cold temperatures, many owners get their dogs a coat. There are many styles to choose from, including ones with Velcro

fastenings, which are very easy to get on and off. Sweaters are comfy but usually a bit more difficult to get on and off, as you need to maneuver the Boxer's long front legs through the sleeves.
- ✔ Halter: One of the newest items in dog training is the halter, also known as the headcollar. This is the same kind of halter a horse wears. The advantage is that the Boxer can't yank and pull against it, dragging you down the street. There is only one position that he will find comfortable, and that is by your side, walking politely. If he tries to pull ahead, the halter turns his head sideways. The halter discourages pulling without any stress to the dog or the walker. Two brand names are Gentle Leader and Halti, but there are many.

Lambskin fleece and faux lambskin beds are great, but inexpensive blankets work as well. Any kind of bed will do.

Of course, the bed your Boxer will like most is your bed. It's your decision whether or not he gets to sleep there. But keep in mind that the cute 12-pound puppy is one day going to be a 60-pound adult. He may be fun to cuddle when he's little, but a full-grown Boxer takes up as much room in the bed as a human, sometimes more.

Kennel crate A crate is a great idea for your Boxer. It's a place where he can rest for short periods and feel safe. There are so many hazards in a home that we never think about: wall sockets, electrical wires, computer cords, chewable shoes, poisonous plants, cleaning materials, toilet brushes, and more. Boxer puppies left alone are prone to explore and pick up everything with their mouths. Boxer puppies in their crates don't get into trouble. They play with their toys and take a nap. They can't destroy valuable curtains or pee on the expensive carpet. A puppy can stay about four or five hours in his crate, but someone should be on hand to let him out if you are gone for longer than that. Take his collar off when he goes into the crate so it won't catch on anything and he won't get his foot caught in it while scratching an itch.

Owners constantly debate whether hard-sided crates, made of plastic or wood are best, or if wire cages are better. Both types have advantages.

Crates with hard sides keep out drafts and more closely resemble the den-like setting of wild dogs. If you transport your dog on an airline, this kind of crate is required.

With wire cages, air passes through freely so they stay cooler on a warm day. In winter, particularly if the wire cage is in a drafty corner, you'll need to drape heavy blankets over it to cover the sides. Wire cages generally fold flat for easy storage.

Whichever one you choose, place the crate in the kitchen, your bedroom, or the living room. Your Boxer likes to be able to see and hear his family. He feels he is your guardian and needs to keep track of who's coming and going. Don't put the crate in the basement, the garage, or the back porch, where he'll be isolated and alone. That will seem like punishment, and he won't want to go in the crate. If forced, he'll feel unhappy and desperate to get out. Provide a comfortable blanket, cushion, or pad so the crate is a cozy place he likes, more like a bedroom than a prison cell.

There is a third crate option, soft-sided nylon mesh or canvas crates that are lightweight and fold down easily. These are a real boon if you are traveling with an adult Boxer. You can take your Boxer wherever you go, and if you need to confine him, pop it out. It has strap handles so you can carry it over your shoulder or tucked under your arm. But don't try to use a soft crate with a puppy, unless he is very well behaved. Puppies get bored and chew on the material, sometimes shredding the sides and destroying the zippers. Wait until he's an adult and thoroughly accustomed to being crated before you try a soft crate.

Various suppliers call these dog bags, dog tents, and soft crates. For most Boxers, the large size is sufficient, as it is used only for temporary confinement. They also come in extra-large and giant. They can be quite fancy and come in many different colors and fabrics. They usually have mesh venting at both ends, so the dog gets plenty of fresh air.

Brushes and combs New owners always worry about getting the right kind of dog brush. A soft bristle brush is best. It loosens any dead hair and massages the skin.

Many people prefer to use a grooming glove, which fits over the hand and makes the process very easy. But this is an optional item; a brush is equally good at removing dead hair. If you run the grooming glove across chairs and sofas, it wipes away any dog hair. Boxers don't shed much, but you will notice white Boxer hairs against dark fabric.

Nail clippers and styptic powder Boxer nails are strong and can grow long. You need nail clippers for his monthly pedicure. The most common type is the guillotine style, in which a stainless steel blade slides across an oval opening. A sharp blade cuts quickly through the nail. The other type is scissors style, which pinches a little less because it cuts evenly from both

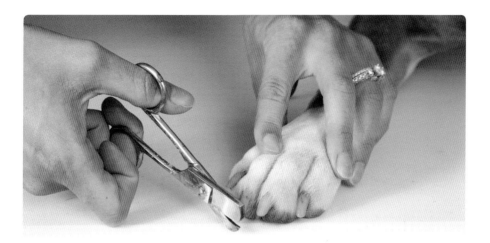

sides. Some people use a nail file. You can purchase one contoured to the shape of dog toes.

Standard styptic powder is used as an aid to stop bleeding caused by clipping nails and minor cuts. Pet stores sell brands specifically for pets, like Kwik Stop.

Another type of pedicure item gaining in popularity is the grinder. The new nail grinders specifically made for dogs make the chore much easier. All dogs hate to have their nails clipped. Only a rare dog will stand still for the process. The new drill grinders are cordless, battery powered, lightweight, and don't make much noise. Most dogs don't mind them. They are a great improvement in canine nail care.

Helpful Hints

Where to Get a Bargain

While pet stores, websites, and department stores have plenty of dog supplies, they can be pricey. If you don't mind a used item, check the classified ads in your newspaper or your local craigslist website, especially for expensive items like chain-link kennel runs, doghouses, exercise pens, and crates.

Chewable items Small pieces of rawhide are the best way to keep his teeth clean. A veterinary school study done over the course of ten years proved that dogs who chew rawhide have cleaner teeth than dogs who eat crunchy biscuits and dogs who never get chew toys. That's because as your dog chews, he massages his gums and cleans particles of food off his teeth. Clean teeth last longer.

Toys Boxers need big, tough toys. They have strong jaws and teeth, and most enjoy tearing a toy apart. Rag dolls and stuffed animals won't last long around a young Boxer. Fortunately, pet stores are full of suitable toys. Rope toys are great for tug-of-war. Kongs and similar substantial toys are excellent. Toys that can be stuffed with treats will provide him with hours of entertainment.

Bones Bones from the supermarket are a great treat, and a great way to keep him happily occupied. Many butchers put out bones in various sizes. The Boxer is a big dog and will be happiest with a big bone. Raw knuckle bones are the best and safest beef bones.

Dog toothbrush and toothpaste Boxers are reluctant to let you brush their teeth. You'll need to go slow to accustom him to staying still while you do it. Toothpaste comes in beef and chicken flavors.

Health Check

One of the items to accomplish in the first week is a visit to the veterinarian. Your puppy should get a thorough health check as described in Chapter 3 (see page 35).

Indentification

At the same time, this is a good time to get his microchip. The veterinarian implants it between his shoulder blades with a special needle and syringe. This tiny chip contains a unique identification number that can be read by veterinarians and animal control officers or anyone with a microchip reader. It's very important to have your puppy microchipped. At present, the chip contains only a number. It's possible to get Global Positioning System devices that you can attach to his collar that will always tell you where he is. They are similar to the ones currently placed in cars, just much smaller.

Once the microchip is implanted, you must register it. When the chip is read, the number will indicate that you are the owner. If you don't register it, it doesn't work to protect your dog. The chip will be read, but the animal control officer will not be able to find you.

The American Kennel Club Companion Animal Recovery service charges a small fee to register your pet for life. There are other microchip registries to choose from. Some charge a yearly fee.

Another method of permanent identification is a tattoo on the inside of the dog's thigh. It doesn't hurt, but it's more difficult to hold a dog still for the several minutes needed to tattoo him than to insert a microchip. The tattoo can also be registered with a national organization so you can be contacted if he's found.

A DNA profile is another means of permanent identification, but is not in general use among pet owners.

Standing Still for Grooming and Examination

Your Boxer needs to trust you and allow himself to be touched and handled without fear or apprehension. Starting from the first day, pick up your puppy and put him on a chair or table.

The first time you do this, most puppies will panic and try to get away. Being up off the ground is not a normal position for them. It feels strange and uncomfortable at first. Stroke him gently and talk to him, telling him he's okay and everything is fine. As soon as he quiets down, say, "*Good boy!*" and put him down. Don't try to keep him for several minutes; if he's scared, he will only feel more scared. This exercise should be done in small, baby steps. When you put him down, he will connect getting what he wants (to be put down) with his relaxed behavior.

Repeat this every day. You can certainly do it more than once a day. If you are consistent, in a few days, it won't scare him. He'll relax, and that is your goal. Run your hands over his body, including his feet. Make it fun by massaging him. Boxers like a good back rub as much as you do.

This will make it easier for him to trust you about other things. It will also teach him to accept the handling that he will get during grooming or from the veterinarian.

CAUTION

Invisible Fences

If you are installing an invisible fence, remember that it only works when your Boxer is wearing the electronic device on his collar. You'll need to follow the directions and take the time to teach him where the fence is and what happens if he tries to cross it—he gets a brief shock.

Boxers respond well to invisible fences, quickly learning the boundaries. They will keep your dog in. But remember that they will not keep other animals out. Loose dogs can come onto your property and start a fight. Squirrels and deer can pass freely and may represent a temptation to chase that causes your Boxer to forget the fence and rush through.

Two Kinds of Walks

There are two kinds of walks. The first is walking in order to relieve himself. For this, walk him on a loose lead or a retractable leash, letting him sniff trees and grass as much as he likes. Allow him a few minutes to find the right spot and do his business. He'll want to stand away from you.

During this walk, you can urge him on by saying, "*Go potty*" or "*Do your business.*" Pick whatever words you like, but associate a phrase with this activity so he'll know when it's time to relieve himself.

The second kind of walk is for exercise or to get somewhere. For this, walk him on a shorter lead so that he has to stay by your side. Tell him "*Let's go,*" and encourage him to walk with you. When he is walking along at your side without stopping, he gets a treat. For this walk, you decide the pace and the direction, not the dog. All Boxers will try to convince you that they absolutely have to stop and sniff constantly, but this is not appropriate. You have already allowed him time to relieve himself. He does not have to do so every few minutes. His job now is to walk with you, stopping only when you do. When he tries to convince you to stop at every light pole and fire hydrant, keep going, giving him a brief tug, and the command "*Let's go.*" He will soon learn to distinguish between the two kinds of walks.

PERSONALITY POINTERS
Boxer Body Language

Boxer Mood	Friendly	Curious or Excited	Playful
Head Carriage	Alert and at attention	Normal posture; wrinkles brow	"Play bow," chest and head lowered to ground, head looking up
Eyes	Wide open	Wide open	Wide open
Ears	Alert, forward or upright	Alert, forward or upright	Alert, forward or upright
Mouth	Closed or relaxed and slightly open in a "smile"	Open, teeth covered with lips, may pant	Closed or slightly open
Body	Relaxed posture or wiggling with excitement	Relaxed posture or wiggling with excitement	Chest lowered to ground, rump elevated
Tail	Wagging rapidly	Wagging	Wagging

If you don't teach your Boxer to walk briskly at your side, ignoring the urge to sniff, you are harming him. No one wants to spend hours walking a dog while he sniffs every tree, so no one will want to walk him. He will end up with only short walks, not proper exercise. If you teach him to walk briskly, you will be able to go at the pace you prefer. A little training makes a walk together much more enjoyable.

What You Need to Know

Your Boxer is a unique being with his own distinctive personality. Boxers are very aware of your body language at all times. They know if you feel happy, irritated, sad, or angry by clues so small you may not be aware of them.

You need to be aware of Boxer body language, as it can tell you a lot about your dog. For instance, a puppy will circle and sniff before he has to relieve himself. If you see him start to do this, get him outside quickly.

Apprehensive or Anxious	Fearful	Subordinate
Neck stiff, head may be pulled back slightly	Head slightly lowered	Head slightly lowered
Wide open, may appear bug-eyed, whites of eyes may show, may have fixed stare	Wide, whites of eyes may show	Partially closed
Pulled back	Pulled back or flattened against skull	Flattened against skull
Closed or slightly open in a tight "grin" with teeth showing	Slightly open, teeth may be visible, may be drooling	Lips pulled back in "grin," may lick or nuzzle
Muscles tightened, movement jumpy	Tense, trembling, body lowered	May roll over on back and expose belly, may also dribble urine in submission
Partially lowered	Tense, still	Tucked tightly against body

He will also let you know when he wants to play, or when his tennis ball has rolled under a sofa where he can't get it and he needs your help. If you start to pay close attention to your Boxer's body language, you will soon become his personal "animal communicator."

The Bored Boxer

A bored Boxer may bark. He may chew on the furniture. He may cry and whimper. The best way to avoid any problem behaviors associated with boredom is to make sure your dog has a generally pleasant and active life, as you do. This means that he needs the following:

- Hugs and attention several times a day
- A comfortable bed to snuggle up in
- An attentive pet parent who he can depend on to take him out to relieve himself
- Walks or play periods in the park or the yard that give him adequate exercise

Separation

A Boxer should be able to accept periods of separation without anxiety. It is normal for humans to be gone to work for eight hours a day. During the hours you are gone, he will be alone. If we observed wild dogs, we would see that they tend to sleep in a safe place for the entire day. They hunt crepuscularly—that is, at dawn and at dusk. A long nap while you are at work is normal for a dog.

Your Boxer needs to be confined when he is home alone, at least for his first year, as outlined earlier in this chapter. If he is free to roam the house, he is free to pee on the carpet, chew your shoes, unplug appliances, nibble on antiques, and get into all kinds of trouble. All of that can be avoided if the puppy has a crate or confined space that is his own. On one side, put his bed and food and water dishes. On the other, put down newspapers where he can relieve himself.

Also leave plenty of toys. Boxers like to chew, and active toys that make him figure out how to get the treats inside are good.

One thing that's very important in crating is your attitude. If the owner thinks crating is punishment and the crate is a prison, the puppy picks that up and becomes worried and nervous, too. He will associate being worried and nervous with his crate. You need a calm, relaxed attitude so you can pass that on to the puppy.

Still, crating can be difficult. Some Boxers exhibit separation anxiety, causing them to cry, bark, or drool constantly. In extreme cases, doctors can prescribe a drug that will make him drowsy and relaxed. The idea is to allow him to experience some time in the crate during which he is not upset and worried. The drug is used short-term as an aid to teaching him to relax.

Of course, exercise is the magic tool to tame a bored Boxer. A long walk will exercise his mind and body and ensure that he is now interested in a quiet sleep period.

Housetraining

Housetraining is a matter of consistency. Your eight-week-old puppy has to go often, so take him out whenever he wakes up. Put him down and use your potty command encouragingly: "*Do your business!*"

As soon as he does, tell him what a clever, wonderful puppy he is and give him a treat. Restrict the puppy's living area to just the kitchen or a corner of the kitchen. It will be easier for you to keep track of him and for him to let you know when he wants to go. The boundaries will aid you in the housetraining process, as Boxers tend to want to keep their living area clean.

Do not give him run of the house at a young age. If he wanders off and pees behind a chair where no one sees, he will assume that it is okay to do so. It's a hard habit to break, so it's best to start on the right foot.

You can teach him to ring a bell when he has to go. Put a bell on the back door and encourage him to touch it. Use a treat to lead his nose to the bell. As soon as he touches it, give him the treat and take him outside. You want him to associate ringing the bell with going outside.

As he gets older, he can wait longer periods between potty breaks. At six months, he can wait about six hours between breaks. Adult Boxers are walked three or four times a day.

Puppy Behaviors

Boxer puppies explore the world through their mouths, picking up every-thing they can reach. Puppy-proof your house by moving the most delicious targets to places where he can't reach them. Put shoes in the closet. Put the remote and cell phones on high shelves. These things look like toys to a young puppy, and he will happily destroy them.

For things that can't be put away, like chair legs and the edges of tables, use bitter apple or a heavy oil, such as lavender, to discourage chewing. Pet stores carry these foul-tasting products designed to prevent this behavior. Even older Boxers can be enthusiastic chewers, so make sure he always has toys to entertain him.

Mouthing

Young puppies will also experiment with mouthing you or your children. You'll want to stop this behavior immediately. It is not okay for a Boxer to mouth, nip, or bite any person, even when he's a puppy. If not stopped, it could lead him to think it's okay to bite people. If he continues this behavior as an adult, it can lead to dangerous situations for you and your Boxer.

Puppies who are raised well and socialized properly by a caring breeder have an advantage. They are kept with the dam until she decides she needs a break, usually when the puppies are about five or six weeks old. Then, she will return to them a few times a day, teaching them valuable lessons on how to behave. If they get into rough play, pulling on mom's ears or mouthing her legs and lips, she lets them know immediately that it's not okay by growling. If necessary, she will nip the puppy to teach him to cut it out. Mom won't put up with being hurt, and the puppy who has been disciplined by his dam learns to be gentle.

Once the dam weans them, puppies continue to learn good behavior by playing with each other in these early weeks. If one puppy gets too rough and bites, the other puppy screams and bites him back. Then he stops the game. In this way, puppies learn to inhibit their biting and be gentle with their playmates.

You, the new owner, need to continue the puppy's learning curve. As soon as he starts to mouth your hand, make a loud noise—"*Ouch!*"—to startle him. Get up and leave. He must learn that if he bites, the game is over. Return after a few minutes and start to play again. If he bites, again make an unpleasant noise and leave. He'll quickly learn that biting people is no fun. If you bite people, they go away and you are lonely. Make sure he has plenty of toys. He'll learn it's okay to bite toys.

There is nothing more important than teaching your puppy not to bite. If he thinks biting is okay, he may bite your kids or visitors. If he bites a stranger, it may lead to medical bills, a lawsuit, or confiscation by an animal control officer. Laws to that effect are set up to protect the public from dangerous dogs. You may know that your dog is only biting in play or not biting hard, but the law doesn't make exceptions. Stop this behavior from the start.

Helpful Hints

Jumping

Puppies enjoy greeting guests enthusiastically, which includes jumping up on them. It's a minor annoyance when he's a little puppy. But a full-grown 65-pound Boxer who jumps on people is a problem.

Treats

Treats will help you shape your puppy's behavior by rewarding him when he does the right thing. Carry them with you when possible. Choose small treats that he can eat quickly.

Whenever he jumps up, quickly turn your back and ignore him completely. Walk away. When you come back, if he jumps, repeat the action, turning away and ignoring him again. Only when he does not jump, quickly reach down to pet him and say hello. You want him to understand that he will only receive attention when all four feet are on the ground. Jumping will get him no attention at all.

To reinforce his training, recruit some volunteers to act as guests. If he jumps when they come in, they should turn and ignore him and then leave. He gets attention only when he's behaving.

In the training chapter, you'll learn to teach him the *wait* command (see page 120). Prepare for this lesson by teaching him from the start that he will never get a treat unless all four feet are on the ground. When you get out a

Keeping Him Warm

Boxers like coats. The breed is extremely sensitive to temperature because of its short hair. In cold weather, most Boxers will welcome a coat to keep them warm.

Many kinds of coats are available. It's a good idea to take your Boxer to the store and fit him with the right one. Because of their deep chests, Boxers will not be able to wear all coats.

dog treat, hold it until all four feet are on the ground, then quickly give it to him. You are teaching him an important lesson in self-control But don't expect him to stand still yet; that's a behavior you'll have to work at over time.

Dog Walkers, Pet Sitters, and Doggie Daycare

Dog walkers and pet sitters visit your dog in your home, maintaining your routine as much as possible. Hiring a dog walker or pet sitter to care for your Boxer gives you peace of mind, knowing someone is there after a few hours to make sure he's okay and tend to his needs.

Pet sitters and dog walkers generally spend about 20 minutes with each client. The exact amount of time should be worked out beforehand. Rates vary across the country in the range of

$12 to $20 per visit. You may be able to arrange for the pet sitter to take your dog to his veterinarian or grooming appointment.

Doggie daycare works the same way as daycare for children. You drop the dog off on your way to work and pick him up on your way home. This is a flourishing industry, with new places popping up constantly. While it's pricey, it gives the owner peace of mind to know that the dog isn't at home chewing the furniture. At daycare, he has playtime with other dogs, snacks, fresh water, and exercise. It's an excellent choice for dogs who are lonely or bored or those with an abundance of energy.

The best way to find any of these services is through recommendations from other pet owners. Business cards are often posted at veterinary clinics. Ask at the veterinarian's office, as many veterinary techs supplement their income through dog walking and pet sitting.

In case he gets lost while under someone else's care, make sure your Boxer always wears a collar with an identification tag bearing your phone number. Keep his license up-to-date. Make sure you register his microchip with a national agency, and keep your phone number and address current so that shelter personnel can contact you.

Breed Needs

Caring for Brachycephalic Breeds

Brachycephalic breeds such as the Boxer are more prone to overheating and breathing problems than breeds with long, wolflike muzzles. Some Boxers have smaller nasal passages, narrower windpipes, or elongated soft palates, which can cause heavy panting, snoring, and snorting. Veterinarians take special precautions when administering anesthesia in order to perform surgery.

Canines cool their bodies by panting, which Boxers don't do as efficiently as longer-nosed breeds. Therefore, it's important to make sure they aren't too hot in the summer or too overheated from exercise.

Brachycephalic breeds have 42 teeth, just as all dogs do, but because the jaw is shortened, sometimes their teeth are misaligned or pushing against each other. This can trap food, which means they need their teeth brushed, as outlined earlier in this chapter. For thorough dental cleanings, the veterinarian has to put them under anesthesia.

The Boxer's facial wrinkles should be kept clean, even though they are not deep and are rarely a source of problems. Problem wrinkles are ones that trap dirt and moisture and irritate the skin.

The eyelid should close all the way. If it cannot, red or dry eyes may need to be treated. If the eyes tear too much, resulting in constant wetness, consult your veterinarian about the problem.

Chapter Five

Living with
a Boxer

When you and your Boxer are together, you'll find him sweet and lovable. He will be an entertaining companion, a friend you can always count on to be there and make you feel better. Boxers are generally able to establish close, trusting relationships with everyone in the family.

That's not to say your Boxer will always do exactly as he's told. Boxers are extremely clever, but they often have their own opinions, which may differ from yours. As one owner says, "My Boxer is beautiful, charming, funny, loyal, and loving. But only when she feels like it."

Your Boxer is never going to talk, but he is trying all the time to communicate with you. He'll never say, "There's a stranger in the yard!" But an owner who pays attention will know when the dog is communicating exactly that.

The Human-Boxer Bond

Dog ownership has increased exponentially in recent years. One reason may be that we have far fewer interactions with other people. Instead of making a trip to the corner store, we e-mail an order and get a delivery. Gone are the friendly exchanges with a human bank teller. There's no need to stop into shops for clothing or purses or stationery, when it's so easy to order what we need online. Some of us telecommute so we don't even have to leave the house to go to work. If you don't have coworkers to laugh with and bank tellers who know your name, the world starts to be a lonely place. Your Boxer is willing to do his part to fill that void.

Boxers have emerged as one of the ten most popular breeds among dog owners and it's not hard to understand why. Boxers are emotional and supportive. They offer the opportunity to give and receive love, without reservation or compromise. Boxers never shame, scold, or belittle. They don't take part in family arguments. In fact, your Boxer may show you that arguments affect him deeply. His head droops; he goes to his bed; he obviously feels sad. He seems to be saying, "Please don't fight. It upsets me."

 Fun Facts

Surveys by the American Animal Hospital Association found that 86 percent of all pet owners include their pets in holiday celebrations; 70 percent sign their pet's name on greeting cards; 58 percent include their pets in family and holiday portraits; and 39 percent say they have more photos of their pet than of their spouse or significant other.

Humans are hardwired to nurture children, puppies, and any small and vulnerable creature who needs our help. Brachycephalic breeds like Boxers tend to inspire this feeling even more strongly because of their almost human facial features. When we rub or hug a Boxer, the power of touch breaks up pain signals going to the brain. Having a dog who needs a walk gets us outdoors and exercising—things known to be beneficial to health.

Boxers are wonderful grief counselors. They were among the one hundred specially trained dogs employed in the support center at Ground Zero after 9/11. They provided solace to those who lost parents, spouses, siblings, and children when the Twin Towers collapsed. Working in two-hour shifts, they greeted and comforted every person who needed them. Six hundred people came to the center each day. One wife said, "With the dogs, for a few minutes you forget your troubles even as you are going up to apply for death certificates. The dogs don't ask anything of you. They don't ask you any questions; they don't give you any advice. They are just there."

Boxers also play a wonderful role as canine nurses to those with long-term illnesses. When he was diagnosed with AIDS, doctors told Harold Campbell that he had 18 months to live. Hal sunk into a terrible depression, but his Boxer, Torch, wouldn't hear of moping around. He insisted there was joy to find in every day. Bone cancer eventually claimed one of Torch's rear legs, but he remained active and happy, modeling for Hal how to live fully in spite of physical infirmity. When Torch died, Hal was devastated and didn't think he'd want another Boxer. But remembering Torch's spirit, he realized the Boxer had always lived life to the fullest and would want Hal to do so as well. With another Boxer, Penny, now by his side, Hal has outlived predictions of his death by almost ten years.

Having a dog who loves you unconditionally, and accepts unconditional love from you, can really ease stress. Since stress and anxiety have been shown to weaken the body and allow other problems to flourish, your Boxer can be just what the doctor ordered to keep you well.

Boxers have a healing effect on their owners, and they can have the same effect on others. That's the basis of the therapy dog movement, in which people take dogs to nursing homes or hospitals. Dogs generally spend just five or ten minutes with a patient, but that little visit brings warmth and happiness to the hospital room. Patients often have pleasant memories of their own dogs they want to share. Visiting the sick is a wonderful way to spend time with your Boxer. As Gay Cropper of the therapy dog group Angel on a Leash in New York City says, "It's just a small thing. But it means so much."

Humans need exercise, emotional support, mental stimulation, and laughter to stay well. Living with a Boxer puts all of those things in your life!

Fun Facts

According to an American Kennel Club survey:

- 97 percent of dog owners would evacuate their pets with them from a hurricane.
- 62 percent would refuse to evacuate if they could not take their pets.
- 66 percent wouldn't even consider dating someone who didn't like their dog.

What Your Boxer Would Say If He Could Talk

If your Boxer could talk, one of the first things he'd tell you is that, in order to be a good dog, he needs exercise. Since he is a big, strong, lively fellow, daily exercise is very important. Fortunately, this is something the two of you can share. Daily exercise will be every bit as good for you as it is for him.

If you have a fenced yard or access to a dog park, you can exercise him by throwing a tennis ball, Frisbee, or toy for him to chase. Boxers love to run, so he will take off at top speed to get whatever you throw. Boxers are not so good at giving the item back, however. A Boxer's idea of a good time is to bring you the toy for a game of tug-of-war that he eventually wins.

If you are keeping a Boxer in an apartment, he needs three long walks every day. If you work during the day, you can do the morning and evening walks. In the afternoon, hire one of the many dog walkers whose cards are posted in the grocery store, pet store, and veterinarian's office. Or put up your own ad, seeking a dog walker. The Internet is a good place to find or advertise for dogwalkers, either in the local classified ads or a listing service like craigslist. Older children in your neighborhood are potential dog walkers, as are members of the family who could use the exercise.

One Boxer person says, "I just acquired my daughter's Boxer on loan. We're both old dogs. He's 10 and I'm, uh, well, somewhat older. He's already brought new vigor to my household. He got me out for an hour's walk in the cold yesterday, something I've not done before. Not only that, but I lost five pounds since he's been on the premises."

Walking a dog is also a great way to meet your neighbors. People are far more likely to talk to a person with a dog than a person walking alone. Everyone has stories about their own dog they want to share. Another dog owner is a great source of tips about what to feed or what veterinarian to visit. Having a dog means you always have a topic of conversation that never runs dry.

He would also tell you that, in addition to being intelligent, he is sensitive and highly emotional. Your Boxer makes an effort to understand you as well as he can. Unfortunately, many of us don't take the time to learn to communicate with him. Even well-meaning owners sometimes don't realize the importance of communication, including nonverbal communication, in establishing a great relationship with their dogs.

Boxer Body Language

Canine communication takes a variety of forms. Dogs use certain body movements and different vocalizations to send signals. Canines communicate with movements of the eyes, eyebrows, ears, mouth, head, tail, and entire body. They communicate vocally with barks, growls, whines, whimpers, and howls.

From your Boxer's body language, you can learn whether he feels excitement, anticipation, playfulness, contentment, happiness, self-confidence,

anxiety, questioning, tentative, reassuring, uncertain, apprehensive, challenging, or submissive. For example, Boxers are so glad to see their owners when they get home from work that they often wag their entire body. Some will lie on their backs and wiggle to signal that they need a belly rub.

Boxer Noises

Barks Boxers bark for many reasons. By listening to your dog's bark, you'll gradually learn what each one indicates.

Boxer barks are not as full of information as a human sentence, but they are certainly more than mere noise. Because Boxers were used as sentries, early developers of the breed wanted dogs who barked a warning that an unfamiliar person was in the area.

Helpful Hints

There are also training tools for Boxers who bark too much, such as collars that release a small amount of lemon scent that dogs don't like, or collars that send an ultra-high-frequency signal back to the dog when he barks. This is annoying to the dog, but it doesn't hurt him. He learns that he can stop the sound by not barking.

Boxers always have a reason for barking, but not always one you can figure out. They bark to attract attention, to communicate a message, or to express excitement. Boxers bark when strangers, dogs, or other animals approach. They bark when they hear an unfamiliar or unidentified noise. They bark when seeing something unexpected. They sometimes bark while playing.

Play barks are often short and sharp, an attempt to get a person or another dog to play. Boxers are brave and not afraid of conflict. Their vocalizations help communicate to other dogs whether they mean harm or are in a playful mood.

The bark of distress is high-pitched and repetitive. It gets higher in pitch as the dog becomes more upset. A dog at home alone might bark in such a way.

A Boxer will often give a warning bark about something he feels needs your attention, as if saying, "Hey, somebody's at the door!" or "A car just pulled into our driveway!" A warning bark will usually start out as a low, quiet growl before escalating in volume.

Barking can be a problem behavior if you have close neighbors. No one likes to be kept awake by a barking dog. Different kinds of barking often require different methods to stop them, so figure out why he's barking before you decide what to do about it. Remember, a dog who barks is attempting to communicate something, whether anxiety, discomfort, friendliness, assertiveness, loneliness, warning, alarm, or something else.

Growls can be used to threaten, invite play, or show dominance. Growling should be watched with special attention because it can be the beginning of a bad behavior, such as snapping at someone. A soft, low growl often indicates the dog feels threatened and may attack if provoked any further. An intense growl, showing teeth, means the dog is very angry and will take action. Pay attention to the message in your dog's growls.

Howls Howling provides long-range communication with other dogs. You won't necessarily hear another dog howling, but your Boxer will. His hearing is far keener than yours. Sometimes dogs howl in response to high-pitched or loud noises such as alarms, sirens, music, or singing.

Whines and whimpers Dogs whine to attract your attention. They whimper to let you know they are in pain or they are afraid of something, such as a bigger dog.

Snarls Dogs snarl by retracting their lips. This means trouble is brewing and requires your immediate involvement.

Vocalizations In addition to barking, some Boxers use a guttural sound to "talk," sometimes when they want something, sometimes when they stretch out on the sofa after a good meal, and sometimes to express contentment at being petted, to say they appreciate the attention.

The Boxer Sensory World

When living with a Boxer, it's helpful to understand their sensory abilities, which differ from ours. They are clever and have an uncanny ability to read our minds. Mostly, they are able to read us through their highly developed senses. They are canine scientists, studying our body language and movements and learning what they mean. In addition, they seem to have a sixth sense that allows them to anticipate our next move.

Sight Dogs' eyesight is calibrated to detect movement at greater distances than we can. But they can't see as well close-up. They can see well in very little light, but they can't see as many colors as we can.

Hearing Dogs hear about four times better than humans. They can detect high-pitched sounds, which is why dogs sometimes howl when we hear nothing at all. Boxers hear very well. They become alert when they hear a strange car in the driveway, turning their heads and perking up their ears. They recognize a wide range of familiar sounds. Much of their barking may be stimulated by sounds that they hear from a distance, which are impossible for us to hear.

Smell A dog's sense of smell is highly developed, and he smells many things we don't even notice. That's why Boxers snuffle in the grass and push their noses right up against people's ankles. They are getting a lot of information about what dogs have passed by or where the person has been. Research done at the Florida State University's Sensory Research Institute by Dr. James Walker shows that a dog can smell *10,000 times* better than a human.

Additionally, the vomeronasal gland on the roof of a dog's mouth is something humans don't have at all. This gland connects to the olfactory function of the dog's brain, giving the dog the ability to "taste" scent. Sometimes a dog will become so excited about a scent, such as the scent of a female in heat, that saliva and foam slide around his mouth. This is because of the strong connection between the scent and taste functions. When a Boxer detects an unknown scent, he usually lifts his head and begins to work the odor through his mouth.

Taste Dogs have fewer taste buds than humans, which may be why they eat things that don't look appetizing to us, such as old meat and even dead bugs. Some people say that's why it's okay to feed dogs the same meal night after night, because they are not looking for variety for their taste buds the way we are.

Sometimes dogs "graze" in the grass, pulling out selected strands to chew. Their body is asking for some plant material, and the dog is filling that need. This often leads to vomiting. It may be that there is something uncomfortable in the stomach and the dog needs to vomit to get it out. If he throws up grass and bile, don't rush him to the veterinarian. Instead, wait and observe him. He may have just solved his own little biological problem.

Touch Boxers love to touch and be touched. You will always find him curled up against you. Many Boxers "hug," pressing themselves against their owners. Boxers love to be petted, stroked, tickled, and caressed.

You're the Boss or Your Boxer Is

It is important to socialize your Boxer starting from the moment he arrives. Socialization is the act of introducing your Boxer puppy to new people, dogs, and different situations in a controlled and nonintimidating way. He must learn that he is to accept your friends without barking or growling.

Even dogs who have never lived in the wild still seem to see their family groups as packs, where the hierarchy needs to be clearly established. Among themselves, dogs always establish who is dominant in the group. There can be different dominant dogs in different activities; for instance, one can be dominant in eating, but another is dominant over certain toys. But dogs in packs always know where they stand.

When a Boxer stiffens and seems to be standing on his toes, he is feeling angry and aggressive. This posture is used to give a warning not to come closer, usually to another dog. Interestingly, bigger dogs will often submit to aggressive smaller ones, dropping their tails or heads to show they don't want to fight.

FYI: Communication

Eyebrows: Boxer's eyebrow movements express emotions similar to the way a human's do. Raised eyebrows mean he is showing interest. Lowered eyebrows suggest confusion, concern, or anger. One eyebrow up suggests bewilderment. If he draws his eyebrows together so his eyes are partially closed, he is suspicious or angry.

Ears: Boxers hold their ears upright when alert and drop them when in repose. Ears that are pulled back suggest the dog is uncertain or fearful.

Mouth: Showing teeth is a sign of aggression, a warning not to come closer.

Lips: Many Boxers pull their lips back to expose the teeth in a "smile," a sign of happiness. Puppies smile before an older dog, trying to signal, "Don't hurt me. I'm little and I won't challenge you."

Head Movements: A head carried high shows confidence and good health. A dropped head means the dog is not well, sad, or unsure.

Tail: Boxers tend to wag their entire rear end when happy or excited. Even if the tail is cropped, it still gives a good indication of his mood. Fast tail wags mean he's happy. Small, slow wags indicate he's not sure of how he should react. High tail carriage indicates a confident, happy dog. A lower tail can be a sign that the dog is submissive or feels insecure.

Body Movements: When a dog stiffens and seems to be standing on his toes, his hair standing out from his body, he feels angry and aggressive. A dog who doesn't want to fight will carry his head lower than the other dog's and his tail lower, too, even if he's wagging it.

It's important for your Boxer to know that you are the leader and will set the rules. One way to enforce this is to use time outs. If he jumps on family members or challenges you, he has to spend a few minutes in his crate, by himself. If he still doesn't calm down, he has to go back in for another minute. Eventually, he will learn to calm down.

A dominance problem is when your Boxer understands what you want but refuses to obey. He challenges you. He stands up to you. When this happens with a puppy, you can insist that he go into his crate or come in the house, because he is small and you are bigger. It's clear who gets to set the rules—you. With a fully grown adult dog, it may be better to distract him by dropping your request for one thing and switching to something else, even something really easy, like "Come over here and eat this biscuit." Or take out a dog treat and ask for a *sit*.

A Boxer who is angry about being in his crate can sometimes be distracted by a bone or toy. He starts enjoying the toy until he tires and takes a nap. Hopefully, the toy is more interesting to him than tearing up his blanket.

People who can't show their Boxers calmly and assertively that they are the boss become frustrated. The dog becomes a problem, sometimes to the point that they don't want him. A good home for a problem Boxer is not easy to find. The person who adopts this dog may have to do a lot of training to rehabilitate him.

Separation Anxiety

Some Boxers have separation anxiety, which means they become anxious when separated from their person or family. In response to the stress they feel, the puppy or dog may pick up inappropriate things, like electrical cords or shoes, or scratch at the door, or chew the windowsill or sofa. He's worried about how long you are going to be gone and how long he'll feel alone.

FYI: Why does the Boxer have a funny face?

A German tale relates that when God created the Boxer, he had a normal wolflike muzzle. God was so pleased with the shape, strength, and intelligence of the Boxer that he said, "This is the perfect dog."

A group of shepherd dogs passed by. When the Boxer claimed he was the perfect dog, the shepherds laughed. The Boxer became so enraged that he charged the largest shepherd, and rammed him with his muzzle. But he was so recently made that the clay was not set, and his beautiful long muzzle was squashed.

God said, "Because you are so vain, your punishment shall be that you will go through life with the short nose you created."

That's how the Boxer got his funny face.

There are a number of things to make him feel better. First, try to give him vigorous exercise before you leave for a long period. Take him for a long walk or throw balls or toys for him to chase.

Teaching him self-control can help him calm himself down. Start by teaching *sit* and *stay*. Use *stay* for longer and longer periods while you are at home with him, in the same room. Work up to having him stay lying down next to you for half an hour, while you watch TV or use the computer. If he learns to relax when you are at home there's a better chance he can relax when you're gone. Ask for the *down-stay* when you leave the house.

Using his crate can also help ease separation anxiety. Make it very comfortable so it's a place he likes, with cozy cushions. Give him a bone, Kong, or toy with a treat inside when you leave. This will keep him occupied, and he'll associate your departure with something good. Left to their own devices, dogs sleep much of the day, so the crate will come to feel like his safe bed or den.

A dog with separation anxiety is always wildly excited when his owner returns. Don't reward that by acting excited to see him. Just give him a pat on the head and a calm greeting to show him that your comings and goings are no big deal.

If you're gone for long hours, you may need a dog walker to come during the day to let him out. This is a good way to break up his day. Just be sure to check references!

Breed Truths

Boxer Emotions

Boxers are very emotional. They feel love, sadness, fear, hope, joy, and anger. You can break your Boxer's heart if you seem to prefer another dog to him. But he will always forgive and forget. He'll be back at your side and stay there through trauma and tragedy. Boxers are always ready to give you a second chance. Remember that when you are mad at him.

As a last resort, veterinarians can provide medication for dogs who are so stressed they are in danger of hurting themselves. The idea is to use the pill to make him sleepy and teach him that it's perfectly okay to fall sleep when he's alone. It's not a permanent solution, however. Even with medication, you'll need to employ other techniques to get him used to spending time by himself.

Five Ways to Make Your Boxer Happy

1. **Talk to him.** Your Boxer will be happy if you give him constant feedback about his behavior. When he looks out the window but doesn't bark, tell him what a wonderful, smart, outstanding Boxer he is. Too often, we pay more attention to our dog's bad behavior then his good behavior. You may find yourself telling him to get in his crate, stay away from guests, and stay out of the living room. You will have a much happier Boxer if you reverse this and praise him for his *good* behavior. When he pees at the designated spot in the backyard, tell him you think that's great. If he's resting on his bed and *not* bothering the guests, slip him a word of praise. He'll be happier and your training will be much easier.

2. **Play with him.** Never neglect his need for play and exercise. Giving your Boxer time by himself in the backyard is *not* a substitute. By himself, he won't be exercising. Instead, he'll sniff the trees, look up and down the street, and roll in the grass. He needs you to throw a ball, hike to the park, or go for a jog. Playing with him is a useful way to build your relationship and a good time to work on *sit, wait, okay,* and *give.* Have him sit, and wait while you throw the toy. Then have him fetch it when you say *"Okay,"* and have him *give* when he brings it back to you. Off-leash dog parks and doggie daycare are also good places for him to play.

3. **Don't use harsh discipline.** Hitting your dog will damage your relationship with him,

Breed Needs

Boxers and the Long Hot Summer

Boxers are susceptible to respiratory difficulties and heatstroke, especially in hot, humid, or stuffy conditions. For this reason, Boxers love shade and air conditioning. You may have to adjust your routine to accommodate his lack of heat tolerance. In the summer months, exercise in the early morning or late evening, when it's coolest. Limit his outdoor playtime when the weather is extremely hot and humid. Make sure that any boarding kennel or daycare facility will keep him in a cool room during heat spells. The staff should understand that Boxers have a problem with heat.

FYI: Popular Boxer Names

Top 20 Names for Boys

1. Max	11. Charlie
2. Jake	12. Jack
3. Buddy	13. Harley
4. Bailey	14. Rusty
5. Sam	15. Toby
6. Rocky	16. Murphy
7. Buster	17. Shelby
8. Casey	18. Sparky
9. Cody	19. Barney
10. Duke	20. Winston

Top 20 Names for Girls

1. Maggie	11. Dakota
2. Molly	12. Katie
3. Chloe	13. Annie
4. Sadie	14. Chelsea
5. Lucy	15. Princess
6. Daisy	16. Missy
7. Ginger	17. Sophie
8. Abby	18. Bo
9. Sasha	19. Coco
10. Sandy	20. Tasha

Other Favorite Names for Boxers

Abbott	Clint	Hurry	Mona	Remington	Tango
Alfie	Cole	Jazzy	Nell	Rex	Teak
Axel	Copper	Jenny	Nena	Ringo	Tessie
Baron	Coral	Jessie	Oliver	Rollie	Tigger
Bart	Dahlia	Jewel	Owen	Rosco	Torch
Ben	Daisy	Josie	Pasha	Roxy	Tori
Bigsby	Delta	Kelly	Penny	Ruby	Trapper
Billy	Diva	Kendall	Petra	Ruckus	Trooper
Bo Diddley	Elliot	Kendra	Piper	Sabrina	Troubador
Bracket	Flannery	Lark	Pistol	Samba	Viper
Brett	Flint	Marco	Polo	Sasha	Whisper
Britta	Gretchen	Madison	Primo	Scarlet	Willow
Brogan	Goldie	Madonna	Quincy	Shadow	Winchester
Brucey	Grace	Marcus	Quinn	Sheba	Xena
Burley	Hawkeye	Marius	Radar	Sienna	Zanzibar
Cammy	Higgins	Marshall	Ramsay	Spider	Zelda
Chase	Hooper	Mims	Randy	Striker	Zinger
Cherokee	Hudson	Minnie	Ranger	Talulah	Zippy

sometimes beyond repair. Don't smack him on the nose, hold his muzzle closed, shake him, or pin him. It is not true that if you spare the rod, you spoil the dog. Punish him for bad behavior with your voice, taking away his toy, or giving him a time-out. If your dog is pulling on the leash, stand still. He's pulling because he wants you to go faster, not stop. Show him that pulling creates the wrong result. If he jumps on you, ignore him and walk away. Later, give him a treat

HOME BASICS
How to Take a Really Good Photo of Your Boxer

Boxer photography is one of the most difficult arts to master as Boxers have a hard time holding still. When you are focusing the lens on him, he is not sure what he's done to receive this attention and may become uncomfortable. Most amateur photos of Boxers are of their rumps, because they move out of reach precisely when the camera clicks.

This can be very frustrating, so be sure to laugh. Don't get mad at your Boxer for something he doesn't understand.

You will get dozens more good photographs if you immediately teach your little puppy to *sit* and *stay*. Then, hold a treat against your camera to keep him looking in your direction. If you are trying to pose him with a child or person, put on his leash. Without restraint, he may choose to hop over the person or go behind him just as you compose your shot.

When you have him posed where you want him, if he won't look in your direction, make a sudden, harsh sound to get his attention, like a "meow" or "yeek" or growl. If you want his head turned sideways, have an assistant attract his attention in that direction with a toy or treat. If you're by yourself, throw a toy in the direction you want him to look just before you snap the shot.

Try to avoid using a flash if possible, as it will cause red-eye and dark shadows. Natural light is best, whether indoors or out. If it's very sunny, find a shady spot with the sun behind you.

Also, you'll take the best photos when you get down to his level. That way you'll get the whole dog, rather than just his upturned face.

when all four feet are on the ground. Boxers hate to be ignored so he will learn to drop those behaviors.

4. **Show him affection.** Your Boxer yearns for your affection and will respond happily if you give him a few moments of cuddle time. Trainers in the military observed that their best dogs were not the ones who received the most instruction, but the ones who bonded most strongly with their handlers. Since military men aren't always comfortable

How to Pet a Boxer

Some Boxers dislike being patted on the top of the head. Because they have a short face and big eyes, they will duck away from a hand coming down on them. Show children that it's much easier to approach with a pat on the neck or shoulder, or to bring the hand up to scratch the chin.

with showing affection, the handlers were encouraged to give their charges a full-body brushing at least once a day, to allow the pair some relaxing time together. Your Boxer needs and deserves a few minutes devoted only to him every day.

5. **Stimulate his brain.** Along with his need to exercise and receive affection, your dog needs to keep his brain stimulated, too. Because they are silent companions, we tend to underestimate our dogs' capacity to learn. But a researcher at the University of Munich taught a Border Collie to recognize 800 words. Assistance dogs learn a vocabulary of 90 words to help the handicapped by bringing phones, remote controls, and bottles of water from the fridge. Your dog may know a lot more words than you realize because he listens and makes associations with "car" or "dinner" or "my husband." He'll respond if you teach him the names of things. When you have to leave him alone, he'll enjoy one of the "puzzle" toys that make him figure out how to get the treat inside.

Communicating with Your Boxer

Eyes Communication starts with the eyes. Make sure from puppyhood that your dog will meet your eyes. In a dog's world, if he doesn't have to look directly in your eyes, he doesn't have to obey you. He will regard himself as the dominant partner. Dogs are visual and, with little practice, will learn to watch you. An exercise in Chapter 7 shows you how to get your Boxer to meet your eyes by holding up a treat, telling him "*Look*," and then rewarding him when he does.

Your Boxer has a finely tuned ability to read your eyes, as well. He can tell if you are happy with him, so he can come bouncing toward you, or annoyed with him, in which case he'll probably ignore you and stay away to avoid any harsh words.

Facial Expression Boxers have eyebrows that are more strongly defined than those of most breeds. They raise and lower them, wrinkling their foreheads. Their eyebrow movements usually express the same emotions as a human's eyebrow movements. Raised eyebrows mean he's interested. Bringing the eyebrows down suggests curiosity or confusion. Bringing them tightly down indicates concern or anger. One eyebrow up suggests bewilderment. You have similar facial expressions, and your Boxer will be able to read them on you.

Ears Whether your Boxer's ears are cropped or uncropped, he will use them to indicate his level of attention. The ears are held upright when alert, relaxed when in repose. Ears that are pulled back suggest the dog is unhappy or fearful. A dog whose ears are habitually pulled back feels insecure. He needs constant encouragement and a lot of socialization in many different situations to develop confidence. A self-confident Boxer is less likely to overreact, bite, or cause trouble. You want to encourage confidence in your Boxer from puppyhood, and noting his ear position will give you a quick way to "read" him.

Jaw When dogs show their teeth, it is a sign of aggression; he is warning someone not to come closer. The Boxer has heavy flews, which make it unlikely you would see his teeth, but you would probably hear him growl in this situation. Some Boxers grin, pulling back the lips. This is a sign of intense happiness and is always accompanied by a sparkling, merry look in his eyes.

Head Carriage

A head carried high shows confidence and good health. A dropped head means the dog is sick, sad, or unsure. Humans think it's cute when a Boxer tilts his head far to the side, and many Boxers are photographed this way. The leaning usually indicates extreme curiosity or bewilderment. Photographers get a dog to perform this movement by making a strange sound, such as a meow or shriek.

Tail

Even though a Boxer's tail is very short, it can still indicate his mood. When it's carried high, it indicates a confident, happy dog. A lower tail can be a sign that the dog is submissive or feels insecure.

When the dog is happy or excited, you'll see fast tail wags. Small, slow wags indicate he's not sure of how he should react but is trying to show that he's friendly. Boxers have such short tails that when they're overcome with happiness, they tend to wag their whole rear end.

Chapter Six

Health and Nutrition

I f he's exercised and fed properly, your Boxer will most likely be by your side for ten years or more. Although generally a healthy fellow, he needs your watchful care. As his owner, you are the one who will notice first if he's not feeling well. If he doesn't want to come out of his bed, scratches one spot more than usual, or shakes his head in a strange way, it's up to you to notice and investigate. A dog can't tell you how he feels in words, so you must decode his behavior.

Feeding your Boxer the right diet for his weight and energy level may take some adjusting at first to find the right food. Boxers are energetic, with a higher proportion of lean muscle mass to fat than other dogs their size. That's the reason for their powerful, muscular appearance. It also means there are special considerations about what to feed them.

Your ultimate goal is to keep your Boxer feeling his best at all times.

Choosing a Veterinarian

To be healthy, a Boxer needs the same basic care as all dogs. That means vaccinations and constant attention to keep him free of parasites.

One of the most important people in your dog's life is his veterinarian. The best way to find a good veterinarian is to ask other dog owners for recommendations. They'll know which doctors are caring and willing to listen, and which aren't. It's important that you feel comfortable with the person who will treat your dog. A veterinarian should be willing to listen to you, especially since you know your dog better than anyone else. If you don't like the first veterinary practice you visit, try a different one next time. You'd do this if you were searching for a doctor or dentist for yourself. Use the same care in finding a veterinarian.

When choosing a veterinarian, also make sure to find out the practice's regular hours and what to do if you have an emergency during off hours. Some veterinarians refer nighttime emergencies to clinics that specialize in emergency care. If that's the case, find out where the emergency clinic is located. You don't want to get lost the night your dog is sick and you're upset.

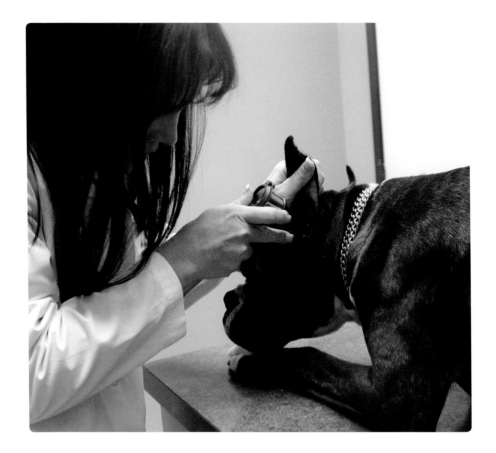

Vaccinations

Your first trip to the veterinarian with a young puppy will be for his vaccination. A puppy gets his first vaccination at around 8 weeks, then at 12 weeks and 16 weeks, although some veterinarians vary that schedule. A puppy gets immunity from his mother through the colostrum he drinks in his first two days of life. The immunity starts to wear off between six to eight weeks, so a vaccination is given. The vaccination protects him from distemper and parvovirus, two devastating illnesses that have caused the deaths of many puppies.

Most veterinarians give combination vaccines. The American Veterinary Medical Association recommends that all dogs receive core vaccines, which include distemper, canine adenovirus-2 (hepatitis and respiratory disease), canine parvovirus-2, and rabies.

Noncore vaccines may be given as well, depending on how common a disease is in your geographical area. Noncore vaccines include leptospirosis, coronavirus, canine parainfluenza, and bordetella (kennel cough). Another possible vaccine is *Borrelia burgdorferi*, which protects against the virus that causes Lyme disease. Your veterinarian will recommend the vaccines that are needed in your area.

When they have reached four months of age, puppies get a vaccination for rabies. Rabies is an inflammation of the brain that is almost always fatal. Unfortunately, rabies is still found in much of the United States, usually spread not through dogs but through wildlife, particularly bats and raccoons. It can occur in any mammal, and every year cases of rabies are reported in skunks, foxes, and coyotes.

Rabies is only spread when the saliva of the infected animal comes in contact with another animal's blood—in other words, only when the rabid animal bites. Rabies shots are very effective. Dogs who have been vaccinated, will not develop the disease, even if bitten by a rabid raccoon.

Because of vaccinations, rabies is no longer the threat it once was. At the turn of the century, more than one hundred people a year died of rabies. Now, it's less than one person per year. In the past twenty years, there have been only ten human deaths. Less than one hundred domestic animals per year get rabies, always from infected wildlife. According to the Centers for Disease Control, approximately 40,000 people come in contact with potentially rabid animals each year, 90 percent of them wildlife. They receive post-exposure prophylaxis, a series of shots that is highly effective.

Rabies vaccinations can be given by appointment in your veterinarian's office. They are also offered for free by most townships or counties once or twice a year. The local animal control officer will have the schedule of rabies clinics.

Parasites

Once your dog is vaccinated, the next thing on the program is the prevention of parasites.

Helpful Hints

What to Tell the Veterinarian

Since your dog can't talk to tell the doctor what's wrong, it's your job to talk for him. Often, your dog won't display the symptoms that you observed at home at the veterinarian's office.

It's upsetting to have a sick dog, which can make you forget something important. That's why it's a good idea to make notes to take with you. Describe what's wrong— he's listless, he hasn't eaten, he's scratching his neck. Be as detailed as possible. It will help the veterinarian with his diagnosis and may cut down on the number of tests that have to be done.

Internal Parasites
Roundworms It is very common for puppies to have worms. In fact, most dogs in the United States carry roundworms latently. They only become active when the dog's immune system is compromised by stress or illness. Roundworms pass from mother to puppies, but the condition is easily treated.

FYI: A Word About Lyme Disease

Lyme disease is carried by the deer tick, a tiny insect sometimes only as big as a pencil dot. When people are bitten, they usually develop a red rash that resembles a bull's-eye. Dogs may not get that symptom. Instead, the first signs in a dog who has been affected are limping and soreness. His temperature rises and he becomes listless. Because this disease is so devastating to the joints, kidneys, and heart, and can lead to neurological disorders, it's best to take limping seriously and have your veterinarian determine the cause. If a blood test shows Lyme, it is treated with a strong course of antibiotics. Even so, relapses can occur months or even years later.

The vaccine against Lyme disease provides some protection, but it is not 100 percent effective in preventing Lyme.

Only when the roundworm infection is advanced do you see the symptoms: vomiting, coughing, malnutrition, loss of appetite, and lethargy. When active, roundworms are often obvious in the puppy's stool, appearing as pieces of white string. Roundworms can sometimes grow to be up to 12 inches (30 cm) in length.

Many medications are available to treat roundworms. Usually a veterinarian prescribes them, but they are also readily available in pet stores.

Heartworm Heartworm is a problem throughout the United States, so heartworm prevention is necessary. The actual number of infected dogs and cats in the country is unknown. Heartworm is most common in the southern states of the east coast, but it has spread to all states, probably carried by traveling canines.

Dogs who have been neglected, abandoned, and picked up by rescue organizations sometimes have quite advanced cases of heartworm, which is spread by infected mosquitoes. When the mosquito bites the dog, tiny larvae called microfilaria enter the bloodstream. They travel to the heart and set up house, growing as long as 14 inches (36 cm). The time from the mosquito bite to the onset of symptoms is about six months.

Most dogs with heartworm infection do not show signs of the disease until it is severe. Symptoms begin with an unexplained cough, followed by decreased appetite, loss of weight, and listlessness. In an advanced case, in which the dog has many adult worms, the dog may die of sudden heart failure.

Heartworm is detected through a blood test, and preventing it is easy with a once-a-month prescription medication. Many heartworm medications are also effective against roundworms. Once a puppy is old enough for heartworm medication, one pill each month can provide protection against all worms.

External Parasites

Fleas Fleas are an annoyance that cause dogs to scratch and bite at their skin. During flea season, medications can be placed between the dog's shoulder blades, killing any flea that bites him. Because the flea life cycle is very short, this solves the problem in a few days.

Some Boxers have flea allergies, which cause excessive scratching. The area of the bite may become red, inflamed, and open to infection. Studies have shown that there are over 15 different antigens in flea saliva, each one capable of causing an allergic response. Fleabite allergies are a common problem, affecting up to 40 percent of all dogs.

Some Boxers are more sensitive to fleas than others. Boxers are not a preferred targets of fleas, as they don't have any warm, moist spots hidden by lots of hair. Even so, Boxers need to be examined periodically for fleas. Preventing fleabites is critical for dogs with flea allergies.

A fleabite allergy will be worse during summer and fall. Dogs will scratch incessantly and bite at the base of their tails. You may notice bald patches or a general thinning of hair. The flea dirt will be obvious if you examine the dog with a flea comb. Severely affected dogs itch their entire bodies, have patches of hair loss, and suffer from red, inflamed skin called hot spots. When the fleas are bad, they will spread to your sofas and carpets, and start to bother humans with their biting.

Ticks In addition to fleas, dogs may carry ticks, which are also blood-sucking parasites. They are found in trees and areas of high grass, so it's important to check your Boxer for ticks after walking in or near woods. Since a Boxer's coat is so short, you can easily see a tick on him. Run your hand over his body. If you find a tick, remove it. A tick needs about 24 hours to impart disease, so if you find it quickly there's a good chance it hasn't harmed him.

Blacklegged ticks, also known as deer ticks, are extremely tiny but can carry Lyme disease, which can cause crippling arthritis in people and dogs. If there are ticks in the area, they will be worse during spring and fall. Use commercially available products that repel both fleas and ticks. If you do find a tick on your dog, don't panic. It's not necessary to rush to the veterinarian. Just remove the tick and watch the spot. Ticks carrying Lyme disease often leave behind a red circle on the dog that resembles a target. If that occurs, do pay a visit to the doctor, as a program of antibiotics is successful against Lyme disease.

Helpful Hints

Tick Removal

A tick bite may be harmful to humans, as ticks sometimes carry several human diseases. If you find an embedded tick, don a pair of latex gloves and, with tweezers, grasp the tick, pull gently until it releases, and then dispose of the live tick by dropping it in a vial of rubbing alcohol. To inhibit infection, it is a good idea to treat the tick lesion by applying alcohol or hydrogen peroxide twice daily for three days.

Allergies

Just like people, Boxers can develop allergies to pollens, molds, and foods. The dog's immune system starts to overreact to a particular foreign substance by producing antibodies that target the allergen. Instead of a stuffy nose and itchy eyes, Boxers get skin irritations, mostly around the head, feet, and belly.

The dog's reaction to allergies is to lick and scratch, which can lead to rashes and infections. If your Boxer develops an allergy, take notes about when the problem started and anything that seems to make it worse. The veterinarian will need to establish the cause of the allergy to successfully treat it. Antihistamines and corticosteroids are often prescribed to reduce the itching and inflammation. But doctors don't recommend ongoing use of steroids. It's better to find the cause and eliminate it from the dog's environment or food, if possible.

If the allergy is to food, you'll need to try various dog foods to find out which one works best for him. With so many choices available, chances are good that you can find a food that suits him. You can switch among various kinds of meat-based foods, such as beef, chicken, turkey, lamb, duck, salmon, and venison. If you eliminate meat as the cause, try dog foods without grain, as this may also be the source of the allergy. Per federal regulations, every bag of dog food includes an extensive list of its ingredients.

CAUTION

In a survey by a medical association, veterinarians reported that Boxers are one of the dog breeds they see most frequently for health problems, second to the Bulldog.

Signs of Illness

Vomiting

It's not uncommon for Boxers to vomit from time to time. Although it's very upsetting to the owner, it may not be a bad thing. Veterinarian and Boxer owner Dr. Peter Batts says, "Sometimes when a dog vomits, he's not creating a problem, he's solving one." If the dog has eaten something that upsets his stomach, it may be better to vomit it up than continue to digest it. Or, he may simply have a sensitive digestive system.

If your dog vomits once or twice without other symptoms, he may be settling his own stomach. Watch him, but don't rush to the veterinarian. Vomiting becomes a problem when it is constant. When there is nothing left in the stomach to throw up, the vomit will be bile, a yellow fluid. At that point, take your Boxer to a doctor. If vomiting continues, he may become dehydrated, which quickly leads to other medical problems such as loss of kidney function.

Many owners have noticed that a dog will chew up grass and later vomit it out. No one knows exactly why dogs do this. It may be that the grass helps get the offending item out of the dog's stomach. He may be purposely causing himself to vomit to rid his body of something toxic. Or, your Boxer may simply like grass, so he's treating himself to a salad. Owners tend to get upset when their dogs eat grass, but in fact, it's normal.

Dogs are primarily carnivores, or meat eaters. But they are also omnivores, as people are, which means they eat foods of both plant and animal origin. Some Boxers' bodies can digest a wide variety of plants and grains.

Vomiting more than once is an indicator of something more serious. A veterinarian will need to diagnose the problem.

If he's vomiting, don't let him eat. The goal is to let the stomach settle. If the vomiting continues, get a plastic bag to take a sample to the veterinarian. It may help with a diagnosis. Undigested food in the vomit is a sign of overeating, anxiety, or food poisoning. Bile indicates inflammation of the

CHECKLIST

Some Causes of Vomiting

✔ Change of diet

✔ Gobbling food too fast

✔ A particular food allergy

✔ Upset stomach

✔ Stomach obstruction

✔ Gastroenteritis

✔ Heatstroke

✔ Liver disease

✔ Kidney disease

✔ Tumors

✔ Whipworms or roundworms

✔ Giardia

pancreas or bowel. Red blood is a sign of an ulcer. Brownish-black blood indicates a problem in the intestines. A strong odor may be a sign of an intestinal obstruction.

The treatment your veterinarian recommends will differ according to what the underlying cause is. Some possible treatments might be:

- Change of diet
- Medication, such as cimetidine
- Antibiotics, if bacterial ulcers are suspected
- Steroids to treat inflammatory bowel disease
- X-ray and then surgery if the cause is a blockage or tumor

Most of the time, the veterinarian will suspect a simple upset stomach. The treatment is often to withhold food for several hours. Make the dog small meals of boiled white rice mixed with plain cooked chicken. Cottage cheese, yogurt, boiled turkey, or a scrambled egg will also be easy for him to digest. Pay close attention to make sure he's improving. If he's not, return to the veterinarian for a follow-up.

Loose Stool

A puppy or dog's stool should be firm and well formed. Loose stool is the most immediate indication that your Boxer isn't feeling well. It can have many causes, but the usual cause is a change of diet. Maybe you switched him to a different dog food and his system isn't used to it yet. Or he ate something rich or fatty. If you haven't fed him anything new, don't assume that no one else in the family hasn't. Boxers have a way of convincing their family members that they are starving. Stress is another possible cause, particularly the stress of moving to a new home.

If your dog has a loose stool, withhold food. You can administer an anti-diarrheal product such as Kaopectate or Imodium. For Kaopectate, the recommended dosage is a teaspoonful per 5 pounds of body weight.

Use a syringe to squirt the liquid into the side of his mouth so he can swallow it. Don't force it directly down his throat, which could choke him and cause him to cough. Let the medicine dribble into his mouth so he can swallow it. If he'll eat yogurt, this could be helpful as well.

If he continues to have loose stools after 24 to 36 hours, consult your veterinarian.

Other possible causes of loose stools are microscopic parasites.

Coccidia Coccidia is a single-cell organism that infects the intestine. These microscopic parasites are not visible to the naked eye but are easily detected by a fecal test. Coccidia cause a watery diarrhea, which is sometimes bloody. It is easily treated by medication. Coccidia is very common in puppies. Researchers have found coccidia in the stools of approximately half of all puppies during their first few months of life. Most adult dogs have reasonably good immunity to coccidia, so they don't develop it.

Giardia Giardia is another protozoan parasite that is a common cause of loose stool in dogs. These small parasites live in any moist, shady area and can be hard to detect. Sometimes they are not even present in the stool of an infected dog. Repeated fecal exams may be necessary to confirm the diagnosis. Signs of giardia include weight loss, inability to gain weight, diarrhea, vomiting, lack of appetite, and greasy-appearing stools. The most commonly used medication for giardia infection is metronidazole (Flagyl), which treats the problem quickly. Giardia is a zoonose, one of the few diseases that affects both canines and humans, so be sure to wash your hands after handling an infected puppy or dog.

Once coccidia and giardia are present in the environment, it is almost impossible to get rid of them. They can hide in even the cleanest kennel. Fortunately, the medication to treat them is effective and lacks harmful side effects.

Common Ailments and Diseases

Bloat

A serious health problem that may affect the Boxer is gastric torsion, also known as bloat. It occurs when an abnormal accumulation of air, fluid, or foam in the stomach causes the stomach to become distended. As the stomach swells, it may rotate, twisting between its fixed attachments at the esophagus and upper intestine. The twisted stomach traps air, food, and water. It obstructs veins in the abdomen, which causes low blood pressure, shock, and damage to internal organs. A bad case of bloat can kill a dog within an hour.

The symptoms can include pacing, whining, nipping at the sides, vomiting, and drooling. There will definitely be major swelling of the abdominal area. If you suspect bloat, get your dog to the veterinarian's office immediately. If the problem is limited to trapped gas, a stomach tube may relieve it. But if the stomach has twisted, surgery is needed.

Bloat is associated with gulping down food, water, or lots of air. For that reason, it's best to feed two small meals a day, rather than one big meal. Some people soak their dogs' kibble in water before letting them eat it.

Bloat is also associated with vigorous exercise, which is best avoided for an hour after he eats. Many people with multiple Boxers enforce a regimen of keeping the dogs in their crates for about an hour before eating, during which time their kibble is soaked in water. The Boxers then eat in their kennels, which is a good way to control the amount each one eats. No one can finish his food fast and steal from his neighbors. Then they are left in the kennels to rest for an hour after eating.

While this is usually a successful strategy, evidence suggests that a tendency to bloat is passed on genetically in canine families. An honest breeder will tell you if bloat has been present anywhere in the family tree. While a dog who has recovered from bloat should certainly never be bred, if the incident occurred when the dog was four or older, he or she may already have produced puppies, inadvertently passing on the tendency.

Dehydration

Because they don't have sweat glands like humans, dogs cool themselves by panting. A dog kept in hot conditions for too long may become dehydrated. Too much exercise on a hot day can cause dehydration, as can a high fever, excessive vomiting, or diarrhea.

Dehydration is the excessive loss of fluids, and it must be treated by the replacement of fluids. When a Boxer becomes dehydrated, the electrolytes in his bodily fluids get out of balance. Chemically, electrolytes are mineral substances, either cations, such as sodium or potassium, or anions, such as chloride and bicarbonate. The balance of the electrolytes is essential for normal function of cells and organs.

FYI: Taking Your Dog's Temperature

A dog's temperature can be taken rectally or in the ear. With a rectal thermometer, use a little lubricant before inserting it about one inch into the dog's rectum. A dog's normal temperature is 101.5°F, although one degree above or below that can be normal. If the temperature is over 102.5°F, take him to the veterinarian.

An ear thermometer works by measuring the infrared heat waves emitted from the eardrum. Carefully place the thermometer deep into the ear canal. A dog's normal ear temperature is 100 to 103°F.

To avoid dehydration, make sure your dog has access to clean, fresh water. Keep a bowl of water accessible to him at all times in the house, yard, and dog pen. Don't let him become overheated.

If you suspect your dog is seriously dehydrated, pick up the loose skin over his withers and hold it away from the muscle for a few seconds. Then release it and watch the time it takes for the skin to return to normal. If it snaps back into place, hydration is probably normal. If it takes more than a heartbeat to ease back into normal position, it probably means the dog lacks subcutaneous tissue fluid and is a sign of dehydration.

FYI: Health Insurance

Veterinary care is expensive, especially when emergency visits or surgery are required. Several insurance companies sell plans for pets. You pay a set amount each month for the coverage and then submit claims paperwork, similar to human health insurance.

It's important to understand exactly what is covered when you sign up. For example, genetic or hereditary diseases and preexisting conditions may not be covered. Monthly premiums vary widely depending on your dog's breed and age, and where you live. Premium plans include wellness exams, vaccinations, and even the most extensive chemotherapy should your dog need it.

Pet health insurance has been popular in Europe for many years. More Americans are now opting for it as the price of veterinary care can be prohibitive.

A seriously dehydrated Boxer should be allowed to drink water in small amounts slowly. Too much water all at once will induce vomiting, adding to the problem. The same electrolyte solutions that are used for dehydrated children can be used for dogs and puppies. If the dog is so dehydrated that he is weak, it may be necessary to dribble small amounts of water into the side of his mouth.

Anesthesia Concerns

Boxers are particularly sensitive to a commonly prescribed tranquilizer called acepromazine. It is often used as a pre-anesthetic before surgery, as well as for tranquilizing dogs in stressful situations.

While it is useful for other breeds, Boxer owners should avoid acepromazine as it has been shown to cause heart arrhythmia and extreme hypotension, a severe lowering of the blood pressure. Other adverse reactions encountered in Boxers include collapse, respiratory arrest, and profound bradycardia, a slow heart rate of less than 60 beats per minute.

Hip Dysplasia

Hip dysplasia affects many breeds and appears to be hereditary, which means that if one of the parents has it, there's a good chance the puppies will have it. It is a disease in which the top of the femur (the hip bone) does not fit properly into the hip joint. Dogs with hip dysplasia experience pain when walking. They don't want vigorous exercise, and they avoid going up and down stairs. In advanced cases, it is very painful.

Hip dysplasia is easily confirmed through X-rays, which can be submitted to the Orthopedic Foundation for Animals (OFA) for an official determination that the dog is free of hip dysplasia. The OFA rates the dog's hips fair, good, or excellent. Many breeders have their dogs x-rayed for this purpose when they reach two years old. An AKC-registered dog's OFA rating appears on his registration papers.

In severe cases, total hip replacement has been very successful. Because the cost is prohibitive, there is an alternate procedure, a femoral head and neck excision. This eliminates hip pain by removing the femoral head and neck and initiating the development of a fibrous false joint. The operation has been successful in alleviating pain and allowing the dog to return to normal walking. The OFA notes that 70 percent of the cases of hip dysplasia respond to a nonsurgical regimen of weight loss, healthy diet, and gentle exercise. Obesity puts extra stress on the joints. Surgery is not recommended if the dog is obese.

A newer method of evaluating hip dysplasia has been developed at the University of Pennsylvania School of Veterinary Medicine. The PennHIP program uses a different method of positioning the dog for the X-ray. Three views are taken, including a compression view, a distraction view, and the standard (OFA) extended view. The dog is assigned a DI or distraction index from 0 to 1.0, with values of 0.3 or below considered not at high risk for developing hip dysplasia. This test can be performed at 16 weeks of age, but it is more reliable if performed later, at one year or after.

Before choosing a puppy, ask, "Have the parents been x-rayed for hip dysplasia?" It's a costly procedure, but it is necessary for any Boxer who will produce puppies.

Breed Truths

As of 2009, 4,660 Boxers' x-rays had been evaluated and rated for hip dysplasia by the Orthopedic Foundation for Animals. Of those, 3.2 percent were graded excellent, meaning they had no evidence of hip dysplasia. Another 10.9 percent were graded dysplastic, meaning they definitely had the disease. The remaining 85 percent of Boxers fell somewhere in between, meaning they showed slight to strong evidence of dysplasia.

Thyroid Disease

The thyroid gland is the largest endocrine gland in the body. It secretes hormones that maintain proper metabolism. Thyroid disease in Boxers develops

CHECKLIST

Health Tests

The American Boxer Club recommends that breeders have their dogs tested for the following conditions before breeding:

✔ Hip/elbow dysplasia
✔ Hypothyroidism
✔ Aortic valve disease

✔ Aortic stenosis
✔ Cardiomyopathy

slowly over a number of years. The disease forms antibodies against the body's own thyroid gland, resulting in the inability to produce adequate thyroid hormone. Boxers with hypothyroid disease may be listless, have patches of thinning hair, gain weight, and be infertile. The simple T4 thyroid test is often inaccurate in identifying it.

Because hypothyroid disease is an inherited condition, check with your dog's breeder to find out if other family members have been diagnosed. An affected Boxer will be put on thyroid medication that he will have to take for the rest of his life to bring his thyroid levels to normal. But, when treated, thyroid problems usually remain controlled and do not inhibit a Boxer's life span.

Heart Disease

Boxers are known to have a predisposition toward certain heart ailments. The Veterinary Medical Database studied 11,000 Boxers brought to veterinary schools over a twenty-year period, from 1981 to 2001. Of those, 11 to 20 percent came in for treatment of heart-related problems, making heart conditions the number-one complaint for the breed. They can be congenital, (present from birth), or acquired later in life. Two types of heart disease affect Boxers, cardiomyopathy and aortic stenosis.

Cardiomyopathy This is one of the most common causes of sudden and unexpected death in Boxers. The condition is characterized by abnormal heart rhythms involving the ventricles, the main blood-pumping chambers of the heart.

Sadly, Boxer cardiomyopathy (BCM) usually has no symptoms. One moment the dog is fine, the next, he collapses, and possibly dies. An expert veterinarian who studies the disease estimates that up to 50 percent of all Boxers are affected by it to some degree.

In lesser cases, there may be symptoms such as lethargy, weakness, fainting spells, coughing, labored breathing, and abdominal swelling. If you notice any sign of symptoms, a trip to the veterinarian is in order right away. The dog may be suffering from cardiac arrhythmias, which can be treated with prescription drugs. Some Boxers can live many years with a good quality of life as long as they take their medication.

Many other Boxers succumb and die without warning, exhibiting no symp-

Helpful Hints

How to Give Medication

Boxers are usually hungry, which is a big plus when you want to give your dog a pill. Simply wrap the pill in a piece of meat, such as ham or bologna, or cheese. Or, cover it with cream cheese or peanut butter.

If for some reason your Boxer is not hungry and those bribes don't work, push the pill to the back of his tongue and hold his muzzle closed until you're sure he's swallow it.

With either method, watch him for a few minutes to make sure the pill is not brought back up.

toms of the disease. When they collapse from cardiomyopathy, a few Boxers recover, but most do not. Males and females are affected in equal numbers. Affected individuals occur in every generation, but two parents who are affected are capable of producing offspring who are not.

The disease occurs when the four chambers of the heart are not working well together. In the upper half of the heart are the right and left atriums. The lower half contains the right and left ventricles. These chambers work together to pump blood through the body. Blood enters the heart at the right atrium and is then pumped to the right ventricle. From the right ventricle, the blood is pumped into the lungs, where it is oxygenated. Then it flows back to the heart through the left atrium, then down into the left ventricle. From there, it begins a journey through the rest of the body.

Valves between the atriums and ventricles regulate the flow of blood. They open to let in blood, then close to keep the blood in for a few seconds. The heart is powered by electrical impulses that are transmitted from the brain. The impulses direct the heart to beat in a steady, regular rhythm. In Boxer cardiomyopathy, these electrical impulses are erratic. They cause arrhythmias, or out-of-sync heartbeats. In a normally functioning heart, there is a pulse at every heartbeat. Arrhythmias are heartbeats that do not have corresponding pulses.

Breed Needs

Now that Boxers' tails are not always docked, they are subject to a condition known as drooped tail or waggers tail. Continuous wagging of a large tail with great force causes muscle damage in the tail about 2 inches (5 cm) from the body. The tail may hang as though broken and it becomes swollen and painful. Veterinarians treat the condition with pain medication and antibiotics, as the damaged area is prone to infection.

If the heart cannot produce a normal contraction, the blood that should be flowing to the brain and body is stopped, causing the dog to collapse. A prolonged run of abnormal contractions can lead to cardiac arrest and death.

Clearly, the best course is to diagnose the disease before any symptoms develop. But Boxer cardiomyopathy can be hard to uncover. An electrocardiogram (ECG) is a three-minute test designed to measure electrical activity in the heart. While it may detect most arrhythmias, Boxer arrhythmias can be intermittent for periods, so the ECG will miss them completely.

Another test often used is the echocardiogram, which is an ultrasound of the heart. It detects whether the heart is contracting properly and shows doctors any thickening of the heart wall. But again, a Boxer can have a normal echocardiogram, yet still have cardiomyopathy that simply didn't show up while the procedure was being done.

The preferred way to evaluate a Boxer is with a portable ECG, called a Holter monitor. Electrodes are placed on the Boxer's body, and he wears the device for 24 hours, during which time the heart's activity is monitored. Because the testing period runs all day, the device will usually detect irregular beats.

Research partially funded by the AKC Canine Health Foundation and American Boxer Charitable Foundation has been phenomenally successful in discovering the mutant gene that is responsible for causing Boxer cardiomyopathy. Kathryn Meurs, an associate professor of cardiovascular medicine at The Ohio University, worked with computer experts at the Massachusetts

BE PREPARED! Possible Signs of Cancer in Dogs

- Unusual bumps on the skin
- Chronic vomiting
- Excessive urination
- Continuous loose stool
- Sores that do not heal
- Difficulty chewing or swallowing

- Lethargy
- Bleeding
- Lack of appetite
- Weight loss
- Nagging cough
- Bad mouth odor

CHECKLIST

Home Health Kit

✔ Thermometer

✔ Heartworm medication

✔ Kaopectate

✔ Syringe to give liquid medication

✔ Phone number of emergency clinic

Institute of Technology (MIT) to look at the DNA samples from thousands of Boxers. They discovered the mutant gene and its placement on the canine genome.

With this information, researchers at Washington State University created a genetic test that can quickly determine the Boxer's risk of death from cardiomyopathy. It is simple and inexpensive, needing only a swab from a Boxer's cheek. This has helped Boxer breeders create breeding programs to minimize—and hopefully eliminate—this disease.

Aortic stenosis This is a constriction of the outflow of oxygenated blood from the left ventricle of the heart to the aorta, where it is transported to all the organs and tissues in the body. The narrowing means the left ventricle has to work harder to pump the necessary amount of blood. The increased workload can result in the thickening of the left heart muscle, as well as increased pressure, which can cause dilation of the aorta.

This physical condition is present from birth, but it is not usually detected in puppies. A systolic murmur becomes clearer in an adult dog. It can lead to heart failure and sudden death. Echocardiograms are used to diagnose the condition, but there is no surgery to remedy it. If mild, it's entirely possible the Boxer can live a normal, healthy life.

Cancer

Boxers are prone to the development of mast cell tumors. If White Boxers aren't protected from the sun, they may develop skin cancer.

Cancer can be genetic, environmental, or a random mutation, similar to how it occurs in people. Mast cell tumors generally form in the skin, creating a bump. The best way to detect them is to carefully look your Boxer over once a week. If you see any abnormal lumps, warts, or swellings, or an area that is painful, a trip to the veterinarian is in order. Other symptoms you might notice include poor appetite, weight loss, and unexplained vomiting and diarrhea.

Diagnosis is usually made by removing fluid from the tumor with a needle, which collects cells. When examined under a microscope, mast cell tumor granules have a distinct stain. Surgery to remove the tumor is done quickly. The healing protocol for Boxers is the same as for humans, and involves chemotherapy and radiation. Advances in medicine have benefited dogs, who can often go on to live many years after a bout with cancer.

Feeding Your Boxer

As pet parents, we try to give our dogs the best food possible. But in fact, they seem happy to eat anything, including goop from the garbage.

Your Boxer's primary food will be kibble. There are so many varieties available in stores that the choice can be somewhat overwhelming. Most of the foods have been specially formulated to meet the needs of canines in various stages of life. The reason there are so many dog foods is that different dogs do best on different types. You will have to experiment to find the best one for your Boxer. The best dog food is one that he likes, does not give him gas, results in small, tight stool, and is easily available for purchase.

The Boxer is designated by some pet food companies as a medium-size dog and as a large dog by others. But, the Boxer is a medium-size dog, weighing roughly 55 to 70 pounds. Weigh your dog; if he won't sit on the scale, weigh yourself, then pick him up and weigh again to calculate his weight from the difference.

Keep in mind that Boxers often have sensitive stomachs. Make sure to choose a highly digestible food, which means a food with a lot of quality proteins. This eliminates the bargain-priced foods that contain a lot of indigestible fillers and result in large, wet stools. You'll want to look for specially formulated dog food. The main ingredient in specially formulated dog food is protein, in the form of beef, chicken, lamb, or fish. Look for these ingredients while choosing your Boxer's food to ensure that it is rich in nutrients and easy to digest. Always buy a small bag of food first and let him try it for a few days. If he likes it, digests

it easily, and produces a small stool, you know it suits him and you can buy a bigger supply.

From Puppy to Adult

The first food your new puppy should eat is the one he's being fed by his breeder. Listen to your breeder's advice on what food to choose. The breeder will know how long to keep a puppy on puppy kibble. Some breeders don't recommend puppy kibble at all. The breeder's advice is based on experience with the puppy's family, so it's the best advice you'll get.

Puppy kibble is made with extra protein and vitamins to help his small body grow to the fullest. Puppy kibble should be more than 20 percent protein and more than 7.2 percent fat. Some go as high as 44 percent protein, which is probably too much. Around 30 percent is probably best.

When he's four months old, switch him over to adult food. He's not an adult yet, but studies have shown that excessive amounts of protein and calcium may contribute to developmental disorders in dogs. Too much protein also exacerbates the development of hip dysplasia. Since the Boxer is a medium-size dog, don't feed him foods intended for large or giant breeds. They may give him more nutrition than his body can handle. An adult food with around 22 to 28 percent protein is best.

When you read a dog food label, check to see that meat is the first ingredient. A good food will have two or three meat listings in the first five ingredients. Since dogs are omnivores, eating both meats and plants, fruit and vegetable ingredients will be good for him. Most kibbles have added vitamins and minerals in a balance meant to maintain optimum health:

- Vitamin A is for healthy eyesight.
- The thyroid needs iodine to function, which may be supplied through sea salt and fish.
- Vitamin B_2, also known as riboflavin, plays an important role in many biochemical reactions in the body, helping with the production of energy from fat.
- L-carnitine plays a major role in cardiac function and metabolism, while iron is an essential constituent in blood.
- Vitamins E and C, taurine, and lutein are antioxidants that combat free radicals.
- Glucosamine and chondroitin aid in the prevention and treatment of arthritis, and are more likely to be found in food for senior dogs.

Food Allergies

Some Boxers develop food allergies, the most common of which is to corn. If your dog isn't doing well on the food he's eating, make sure you get him one without corn. Wheat is the second most common allergen. Other allergies may be to brewer's yeast, artificial flavors, and colorings. Don't go by the word *natural* on the package, as use of the term isn't regulated in pet food as it is in human food.

The meat in dog food is usually beef, chicken, lamb, or turkey. If your dog isn't doing well on one food, switch to another. The meat most commonly indicated in allergies is beef. It's possible to find duck, venison, bison, or fish formulas.

Common signs of food allergies are red itchy skin, ears, or feet; persistent ear infections; diarrhea and vomiting; and bumps on the skin. If you suspect your dog has allergies, choose a food with few grains and only one or two different meat proteins.

Since Boxers are at risk for developing cancer, it's best to avoid foods that contain preservatives linked with cancer risk. The most commonly used chemicals that should be avoided are BHA (butylated hydroxyanisole), BHT (butylated hydroxytoluene), ethoxyquin, and propylene glycol, a cousin to antifreeze, which is found in many semi-moist dog foods.

The number-one reason that adult Boxers visit the veterinarian's office is for heart ailments. Certain foods can play a part in keeping your dog's heart healthy, such as those containing taurine and L-carnitine, antioxidants, and EPA and DHA, which have been shown to promote stable heart function.

Avoiding Bloat

Even when he's fully grown, feed your dog twice a day rather than just once, to avoid the risk of bloat. An adult Boxer eats approximately two cups per meal, for a total of four cups per day. Bloat occurs when a dog gulps too much food with too much air, too fast. For this reason, feed a larger kibble rather than a smaller one so that he has to chew his food. Special dishes with an island in the center can help prevent the dog from shoving his muzzle into the bowl and inhaling large amounts of food. You can achieve the same effect by placing a can or rock in the center of his dish, forcing him to eat around it.

Fun Facts

The yearly amount spent on food for dogs is $5 billion (Petfood Industry publications).

Americans spend about $9.4 billion per year on the health of their pets (American Pet Products Association).

Dog owners spent an average of $785 on veterinary bills (*Smart Money* magazine).

The owner of a typical American dog will spend $11,500 on the animal during his lifetime—half of it on medical care (American Veterinary Medical Association).

When to Switch

When should you switch his food? When a problem arises that has no other known source. He's vomiting, or itching, or passing smelly gas. Eliminating grains is usually the best way to stop smelly Boxer gas, as his system may not be digesting them properly.

One Boxer owner recalls, "When we adopted Rudy six years ago, he had been eating whatever they feed at the shelter. His stool was very runny, his coat was thin, his ears were moist and reddened, he threw up almost daily,

and he scratched himself until he bled on his ears and flanks.

"We switched to a kibble made with potato and duck. After we made the switch, he gradually got better. I still give him Benadryl twice a day on the advice of my veterinarian, to make sure he doesn't itch, but he no longer tears his skin up with scratching."

Homemade Nutrition

As a special treat, many people add canned dog food, leftovers, or cooked meat to make their dogs' food more tantalizing. The Boxer loves his meal, and the preparation appeals to people

CAUTION

Do not feed your Boxer any kind of "lite" or "low fat" weight reduction kibble. If he's getting heavy, simply cut down on the amount he's eating. Fat is a crucial part of a canine diet, and dogs tolerate high fat levels much better than humans. Fat is important for the muscle cells' ability to break down carbohydrates into energy. A high-fat diet improves the Boxer's ability to utilize the fat.

who like to nurture their dogs. Dog food companies spend millions on research to find the perfect blend. But Boxer owners still sometimes like to shop and cook for their dogs, buying expiration date and inexpensive cuts, such as organ meat. Most grocery stores now keep a refrigerated unit in the pet food section, full of specially prepared raw or cooked meat.

Balanced Nutrition

Scientific studies have shown that diets high in carbohydrates and low in fat result in a Boxer who is easily fatigued and has a low energy level. For a robust, energetic, highly active breed like the Boxer, a high proportion of fat is essential. Omega-6 unsaturated fatty acids of the kind found in vegetable oils improve the digestibility and use of energy in the food.

CAUTION

What to Do If Your Dog Eats Chicken Bones

First, don't panic. If the bones upset his stomach, he will most likely throw up. If the bones are raw, they are soft and flexible. He'll probably just digest them and you won't notice anything wrong. Well-cooked bones, like the ones from commercial fast food restaurants such as KFC, crumble and dissolve easily. The problem comes from large bones that are brittle and splinter.

If your Boxer eats bones, monitor him for the next day or so, noticing if he becomes uncomfortable or listless. If he nips at his stomach or strains to defecate, a trip to the veterinarian is in order.

When humans want to lose weight, they cut out butter, oil, mayonnaise, cream, and other fats. But this is not a proper approach for a Boxer. His energy level, coat, and overall health will suffer. Dog foods from reputable companies have balanced fat, protein, and carbohydrates. Give him half a cup less of a good, balanced food, but don't cut out the fat. In fact, if his energy seems low and his coat isn't shining, try adding a tablespoon or two of vegetable oil to his kibble.

Raw Food Diets

A diet of raw food has become very popular in recent years. The diet is called BARF, which stands for "bones and raw food." People whose dogs have many medical problems and are not responding well to treatment and medication sometimes turn to the raw diet, sometimes with good results.

Since dogs were once wild canids who did not cook their food, they are equipped to handle raw meat. Even fussy eaters are known to start eating eagerly when fed a raw diet. The recommended formulation is 60 percent raw meat and bones and 40 percent vegetables and fruits. The raw meat and bones can include chicken backs and necks, turkey necks, venison, and whole fish. Raw beef knucklebones are given as treats for him to chew.

One of the biggest problems with the raw food diet is that it is time-consuming to prepare. Since it's raw, it doesn't travel well. Also, it's necessary to clean constantly and be very careful while preparing it, because raw food contains a lot of bacteria. You don't want that to spread to human food in your kitchen.

For those who want to try a raw diet with their Boxers, there are now companies that package raw meat and also formulas of raw meat mixed with vegetables.

With whatever diet you try, always switch over gradually, adding a little of the new food to the old food the first three days to give his stomach a chance to adjust.

Chapter Seven

Training and Activities

Secrets of Successful Boxer Training

When do you begin a Boxer's training? The moment he comes into your life. How often do you train your Boxer? Every day. If that sounds like a lot of work, you need to change your idea of what training is. It is a way of communicating with your Boxer that is fulfilling and interesting, both to him and to you. From the time he is eight weeks old, start asking him to pay attention, to wait while you open the door, to sit, to come, and to settle down. Praise him when he does as he's told. Show him that working with you is more fun than ignoring you or disobeying.

Boxers are highly intelligent and fun to train. However, that same quick intelligence gives the Boxer a mind of his own. They constantly surprise their owners with unexpected responses. They are also comedians with a great sense of humor. Your best bet is to agree with your Boxer that life is a game and the purpose is to have fun. Indulge him sometimes when he brings your underwear from the laundry or carries your shoes onto the front yard. He's not really being bad—he's entertaining you.

All trainers need patience and persistence. Boxer trainers need a good sense of humor, too.

Should a Boxer Go to School?

One new Boxer owner said she didn't want to take her dog to obedience class because, "I don't want him to be a robot. I just want him to be good in the house."

There's a kind of catch-22 to training a Boxer. Even though you might not care about sitting and heeling, the better he gets at those tasks, the better he will be in the house. The more he uses his mind to figure out what you want, the better behaved he will be. Marching around the obedience class ring is not wasted time. You think you're training him to heel, but he's learning how to listen, how to understand you, and how to do what you want. You are building the foundation for all kinds of good behavior.

ACTIVITIES Where Should You Train Your Boxer?

Where can you find classes to train your Boxer? In today's world, there are many possible answers to that question.

Pet stores. PetSmart, Petco, Pets Plus, and other large pet stores offer training classes that are generally small and scheduled at convenient times. The teachers are usually dedicated and eager to help. These classes are a great place to start your dog's training career.

Dog training schools. Check the Yellow Pages, do a search on *craigslist.com*, or Google "dog training" and the name of your city to find a school. Interest in dog training is high, and new schools are opening all the time. You may find that you can check out several schools and pick the one that will suit you.

Boarding kennels. Boarding kennels that have enough room and enough interest may offer training classes to the public. If they don't give classes, they may have a bulletin board with training schools posted.

Veterinarians. Your veterinarian's office is another potential source of information about local training schools. Many veterinary technicians teach obedience classes in addition to working in the veterinary clinic.

Kennel clubs. Your local kennel club probably holds many training classes. This is a good place to find out about competitions in obedience, rally, and agility. Local kennel clubs are members of the national organization, the American Kennel Club. Look up your city under "Clubs" at the AKC website, *www.akc.org*.

Private in-home trainers. Trainers often post their business cards at the local grocery store or veterinarian's office. The Association of Pet Dog Trainers has a search engine on its website that you can use to find a trainer near you (*www.apdt.com*).

Another good way to find out about training classes is through word of mouth. Ask at a dog park or among other dog owners in your neighborhood.

Training helps a less assertive owner develop the boss/employee relationship that's needed with the Boxer. He must know that you are in charge. The experienced trainers who teach classes can show you how to do that without getting angry or smacking him. They can model for you the attitude and approach you need. You might not think you need help, but if Bucky pushes past you to go out the door, jumps on your friends, and drags you with his leash, you do.

Training Basics

Training does not have to take place at the same place and time every day. Training is part of life. The kitchen is a great place to start, however.

Remember, you are the boss. When you give a command, be firm. Boxers can pick up emotion in your voice. If you say, *"Sit"* in a sweet singsong voice, he will recognize that you are thinking about how cute he is or how much you love him. He will ignore you. When you tell him what to do, mean it.

Don't punish, scold, or yell at him. A Boxer will feel confused and unhappy, and you will lose his cooperation. Say *"Sit"* and if he doesn't, take him by the collar and tell him again. Then reward him with praise and treats when he does it.

Move forward in baby steps. Reward him when he makes a little progress—for instance, sitting on command. He will try to test you by not sitting the next time you ask, so go back to the beginning and show him again what you want. Then reward him again.

Define your terms clearly. Use the word *down* to mean lie down. If you want him to get off the couch or not to jump up on friends, say, *"Off."* You also need a release word to let him know when he can relax. *Okay* or *good boy* are good ones. It means the lesson is over and he can go watch television on the couch with your kids.

Persistence is everything in training. Boxers are smart. If you teach him to *sit* and the next day he pretends he forgot how to do it, don't give up. Teach him again. Then switch to teaching him something else. If you hit a snag, a training class or a visit from a professional trainer may open your eyes to a better way to work with your particular dog.

Your dog is only going to be as well behaved as you teach him to be. He needs your time and attention. Lessons from his childhood will pay off throughout his life.

Basic Commands

The first thing to teach your Boxer is to pay attention. Until you get his attention, you can't teach him any-thing. So start by teaching him the command *look*.

The beauty of the *look* command is that it is the building block of all your other commands. Fortunately, *look* is easy to teach a Boxer at any age. Even five-week-old puppies can learn it.

1. Take a treat in your hand and let him sniff it.
2. Bring the treat up between your eyes and say "*Look.*"
3. As soon as he looks at it, give it to him. Do it about five times, then let him know that he is truly the most brilliant Boxer puppy that ever lived and you are honored to have him in your home.
4. The next training session can be anytime at all, from ten minutes later to the next day, whenever you have a minute and the treats are nearby. Give the command *look*. When he looks at the treat, pause for a second before giving it to him. He must stand still with all four feet on the floor. Then give him the treat. Keep extending the time that he has to hold still and look at you.

This is how show Boxers are taught to hit their stance. The handlers want the dogs to tighten their muscles, stand balanced on all feet, and adopt the breed's typical expression. As soon as your puppy does those things, he gets the treat. He may get so good at it that you decide to show him!

Surprising Sources of Good Training Information

Television. Watching dog trainers on television is an entertaining way to learn new methods. The two most popular dog training shows are Cesar Milan's, *The Dog Whisperer*, on the National Geographic cable channel, and *It's Me or the Dog* with English trainer Victoria Stilwell, on *Animal Planet*. Both trainers deal with a variety of complicated situations. In many cases, they have to untrain dogs from bad habits before instilling better attitudes and new behaviors. It's amazing what they accomplish.

DVDs and videotapes. There are many videos available offering to show you how to train your dog. Most training videos use similar methods: positive, reward-based training without harsh punishments. Among the most popular are Karen Pryor's *Clicker Training* series and *How to Be Your Dog's Best Friend* by the Monks of New Skete. Your first training DVD is the one provided with this book.

The Wait Command

If you can only teach your Boxer one thing, it should be *wait*. A dog who will wait is not going to rush into the street and be hit by a speeding car. He is not going to throw himself at your 80-year-old grandmother and knock her off her walker. He is not going to leap onto the kitchen counter as you are balancing the filet mignon out of the oven. *Wait* is a very handy, very necessary command in your Boxer's life.

Wait is a temporary order. He doesn't have to sit. It's not going to take a long time. He just has to pause until you determine it's okay for him to move forward. It's a very important command. As with all training, you have to use repetition to get the message through. Also, keep in mind that dogs are situational. Don't assume that since he will wait and not rush through *your* front door that he won't rush through anybody else's front door. Take him to a friend's home for a quick training session. This teaches him that he has to generalize. "Wait" means "wait" no matter where he is.

1. Start this lesson in the house, behind a closed door. Open the door, and if he moves forward, block him from going through while you say *"Wait."* You don't need a treat just yet. Food would be a distraction.

2. Open the door again and block him if he tries to go through. To reinforce your verbal command, show him the palm of your hand while you say *"Wait."*
3. Make him wait for just one second and then give the release command, *"Okay!,"* and let him come through the door. Praise and treat.
4. Gradually extend the time that he has to wait. He doesn't have to sit. He doesn't have to lie down. He doesn't have to do anything but stay where he is for a moment.

Come

One of the most important things your Boxer needs to know is that when you call him, he should come. There is no trick to it; like all dog endeavors, it is the result of practicing, day after day, something very simple. Teaching *come* is easiest if you can start when the puppy is young.

1. Take him out in the backyard or to the park, pick him up and carry him to the middle of the field, put him down, play with him, and walk away. Tell him in an encouraging voice *"Bucky, come!"* At that young age, puppies have a built-in instinct to follow.
2. When he follows you for about 10 steps, stop, give him a treat, and play with him. These are the best things in

a puppy's world. Nothing is more fulfilling than treats and play with his owner.

3. Keep walking, tell him *"Bucky, come!,"* and repeat the stops for treats and play. Now and then, he might fall behind or make a bit of a dash in the wrong direction, but he will *always* turn around and come with you.

4. After a brief rest, stride off again. Your puppy will fall into line behind you. After about 20 feet, stop and repeat the treats and playing. Then start off in another direction.

This lesson in freedom is very important in a dog's life. You want your dog to learn that it doesn't matter whether he is on a leash or running free, it is all the same. He will get in the habit of following and coming to you.

With an older puppy or dog, do the exercise with the dog on a retractable lead. This gives him a lot of freedom without worries he will run off. Eventually you can graduate to doing it off leash.

This lesson teaches him that when you call him, he should come. Many people say, "I don't have time for that!" and the answer is—make time.

Time to Go Out

You can train your Boxer to notify you when he has to go out. First, consistently use just one door to take him out to eliminate, so he will associate that door with that project. Then, put a bell on the door at about the level of his nose. Get some treats and encourage him to touch the bell by leading him toward it with a treat. Be patient if he doesn't understand what you want right away. Work in baby steps. Reward him for moving a little closer to the bell. Then hold the next treat until he moves a little closer. When he touches it, no matter how lightly, give him a big payoff of three or four treats and lots of praise: *"Good boy! Smart boy!"* Take him out immediately to the elimination area.

One Boxer owner reports, "I was trying to teach Willy to let me know when he has to go out by pawing the door, but he's ended up pawing me on the leg instead!" This is either a case of training gone slightly awry or yet another example of the famous Boxer sense of humor.

SHOPPING LIST

Training

✔ **Collar.** For a puppy, a simple leather or nylon collar is sufficient. For an older, stronger dog, use a larger leather, or rolled leather collar.

✔ **Leash.** A 6-or 8-foot nylon or leather leash is best.

✔ **Treats.** Hot dogs or string cheese cut into quarter-inch slices make the best treats. Your pet store will have all kinds of packages of treats. Choose ones with small pieces that can be eaten quickly.

Rewards

People work hard to earn their pay. Those on commission work to increase their bonus. Just as people want money, Boxers want treats and praise. It's good to keep in mind that both people and Boxers work harder when they know there's a reward at the end of the task.

What's the best treat?
To achieve the very best motivation, you must offer something truly delicious. For you, that might be Belgian chocolates. For a Boxer, it's meat.

Hot dogs. Buy the cheapest generic hot dogs in the store. Cut them into quarter-inch slices, and put them in a small plastic container that you can keep in the refrigerator. That container needs to be full and in a handy spot, so that every time you give a command, you can pop a treat in his mouth.

Chicken. Many people cut cooked chicken into little pieces to use as rewards, particularly those who tend to park the treat in their own mouths so that both hands are free to direct the dog.

CAUTION

Treats Are Food

If the two of you become an enthusiastic training team, you may have to cut down on the amount you feed him at mealtime because he's consuming so many calories in training treats. You don't want him to become overweight, so cut back on what goes into his bowl.

PERSONALITY POINTERS
Positive Reward Is the Best Approach

Boxers respond best to positive, encouraging teaching methods. Forcing them to do something makes them distrust you. Keep in mind:

- Your Boxer wants you to be happy. You are more fun when you're happy. Your job is to show him what makes you happy. Getting angry just frightens him and makes him harder to train. Be clear about what you want and ask firmly.
- Punishment does not work. It just makes him back away from you.
- Accentuate the positive. Always reward him when he does it right.
- Boxers will usually work for food! He'll be even more responsive if he feels a little hungry. Don't work him immediately after he's eaten.

Liver. For sheer motivational power, there is nothing like liver. Boil or bake it, and let it dry out on paper towels. Liver is so delicious that Boxers open their eyes wide and their mouths salivate when they realize that liver is on offer. Cut it into *very small* pieces, and keep track of how much you've given him. Liver is rich. Too much will give him a tummy ache and loose stool. (When you watch a dog show, either in person or on television, notice how intently the dogs look at their handlers' hands. What keeps the dogs so focused? Liver.)

Store-bought treats. On the pet store shelves, you'll find an endless assortment of training treats. Make sure they are small enough that he can finish the treat in two or three bites.

String cheese. String cheese comes individually packaged as a snack. It works great as a Boxer treat. Give him about a quarter-inch piece at a time.

Beef jerky. You'll always find boxes of beef jerky near the potato chips, nachos, and cupcakes at the supermarket. They make great training treats, in small pieces.

Biscuits. Boxers tend to feel hungry all the time, so biscuits work well as treats. For training purposes, use small biscuits that he can crunch up in two or three bites. A big dog biscuit that takes a lot of work to chew is better as the treat in his crate when he's left alone for a few hours.

Vegetables and fruits. Some people swear that their Boxers like carrots, broccoli, apples, bananas, and grapes. If they do, great, because vegetables and fruits are as good for his health as they are for yours. But like small children who prefer candy, not all Boxers are willing to accept vegetables and fruits as rewards. When you really want to get his attention and ramp up the training, use meat.

The Talented Boxer

Many Boxers are great successes in performance events. The well-trained Boxer is a glorious picture going through his paces in the obedience ring or joyously rushing through the agility course. Occasionally, Boxers are successful in lure coursing, tracking, and other performance pursuits.

Boxers also make wonderful therapy dogs who are much appreciated by the elderly and sick patients that they visit. Boxers also work as service dogs, as guide dogs for the blind, hearing dogs for the deaf, and seizure alert dogs for those who suffer from epilepsy. They perform beautifully as narcotics detectors, police dogs, and in search and rescue operations. The Boxer is always willing to assist his human friends.

Activities

Boxers are fun to show in the breed ring, smart and confident in obedience and rally, and competitive in agility. They make wonderful therapy dogs, delighting patients and charming caregivers. They enjoy taking up a dog sport or pursuing an activity as much as their owners do. Starting an activity is a great way to enhance the bond between you and your Boxer.

Canine Good Citizen

The Canine Good Citizen (CGC) program puts your dog through his paces to see if he is properly socialized. Your dog must be able to perform a series of ten exercises that

Fun Facts

In California, a Boxer named Deja goes on over 40 searches a year as a member of the county Canine Specialized Search Team. In addition to trailing live people, she is a mission-ready cadaver search dog who has found drowning victims underwater 11 times.

In Indiana, a Boxer named Izzy on the Jefferson County, Kentucky, search and rescue team discovered evidence that helped police convict the murderer of a child.

can be learned as part of basic obedience training. The main thrust of the test is to show that your Boxer is even-tempered, well-mannered, and friendly, and never aggressive, shy, or fearful. The tests involve simple obedience exercises: *sit*, *stay*, *down*, loose leash walking, and reaction to distraction and strangers. If you're interested in enrolling your boxer as a therapy dog, completing the CGC test is the first step.

ACTIVITIES Clicker Training Your Boxer

Clicker training is based on a behavioral psychology concept called "operant conditioning." The clicker is used to mark the Boxer's correct action and reward it.

A clicker is a mechanical device that makes a short "click" sound. It tells Bucky when he's doing exactly the right thing. A clicker signal is used because it is fast, noticeable, and something dogs don't encounter in everyday life. The great thing about clicker training is that it gets the Boxer to think for himself.

The first step is to get him to associate the click with a reward. Start by holding the clicker in one hand and treats in the other hand. Now, click and give your dog a treat. Do it again, and again. Click and treat. Within a few minutes, your pet should have this figured out. End the session.

When you first begin clicker training, it's best to keep sessions very short, only five to ten minutes at a time. This way your dog will be able to stay focused, and it will encourage him to think of it as a game.

Once Bucky realizes the click means he gets a treat, you can begin shaping his behaviors. *Sit* is a good place to start. Repeat the *sit* training you used earlier, but this time, click the instant that his bottom hits the ground. Give a treat.

One fairly easy behavior to teach is the *go to bed* command. At first, click any time Bucky looks toward his bed or passes by it. Then, click when he takes even one step toward it. Then start clicking and treating for several steps in the right direction. Eventually require him to go all the way over to the bed. Once he has figured out what you want, add the command "*Go to bed.*" It's not the clicker that's the magic; it's the operant conditioning principles.

For more advanced behaviors you may need to slowly work up to the cue point. For example, you can teach your Boxer to turn in a circle by clicking for any movement he makes in that direction, even if it is only a turn of the head.

Once your Boxer is reliably looking over his shoulder with every click, withhold the click and wait for him to offer a little more. The key is to train in very small baby steps. The smaller you can break things down, the better. Don't require too big a change or he may become confused. If that happens, just step back and start again by rewarding the first small steps.

Therapy

Therapy dogs provide comfort and companionship to patients in hospitals, nursing homes, and other locations where the presence of a calm, happy dog would be beneficial. Research has proven that therapy dogs lower patients' blood pressure and relieve stress and depression. Even very ill patients can benefit from the unconditional love and acceptance provided by therapy dogs.

Sometimes the dog becomes part of the therapy by bringing back a ball to be thrown or being brushed all over his body, exercises designed to get the patient's muscles moving. Some dogs are trained to help stabilize patients who are learning to walk or entice children to their feet for a gentle game.

When Boxers visit nursing homes, some elderly patients are eager to share stories about dogs they knew and loved long ago. Since many of the patients will never be able to experience the joys of dog ownership again, the Boxer provides a link to joyful past experiences.

If volunteering your Boxer as a therapy dog interests you, contact the Delta Society (425-679-5500 or *deltasociety.org*), or Therapy Dogs International (973-252-9800 *or tdi-dog.org*), to find out how your Boxer can become a registered volunteer. He'll have to pass a test similar to the AKC's Canine Good Citizen test, but with added exercises that require the Boxer to interact with people using wheelchairs and walkers, and lying in bed. You will find the training needed to be a therapy dog useful in all aspects of his life.

CAUTION

No-harness Zone

Do *not* subject your Boxer to a harness, except under one condition: You want him to pull a cart. Harnesses were invented so that animals could pull large loads easily. The only large load on the end of the Boxer's leash is you. A harness makes it easier for him to drag you down the street. It gives you no control over him and no ability to direct him. The proper gear for a Boxer is a collar and leash.

One exception: Canine seatbelts are attached to harnesses.

A new opportunity for therapy dogs is helping children as they learn to read. Teachers discovered that children who are struggling to read and embarrassed by their mistakes are more willing to read to dogs than to other children or their parents or teachers. The calm, nonjudgmental presence of the dog gives them confidence. Therapy Dogs International's reading program is a wonderful opportunity for children to interact with and learn about dogs in a positive manner. Because Boxers are good with children, they are a natural match for this duty.

Obedience and Rally

Training for either obedience or rally competition can be fun for both the handler and dog. It's special time spent together, forging an even stronger bond between the two of you. Additionally, the skills learned for the Novice level can serve as an excellent foundation for agility competition and therapy work.

Obedience

Obedience is a competition in which dogs must demonstrate a variety of skills requiring teamwork between dog and handler. The basic objective of obedience trials is to recognize dogs that have been trained to behave in the home, in public places, and in the presence of other dogs. The basic exercises include:

- On- and off-leash heeling
- Standing for exam
- Maintaining a *sit* and a *down* with the handler at a distance or out of sight
- Recall

At the next level, Boxers are required to:

- Drop on recall
- Retrieve on a flat surface and over a jump
- Perform a directed retrieval
- Retrieve an article based on scent

Basic obedience is a great first step before training in agility.

Rally

Rally is the newest of the AKC events. It is intended to be a bridge between the Canine Good Citizen program and formal obedience competition. It allows an inexperienced dog and/or handler to gain ring experience without the stress that can occur in the formal obedience ring.

The rally judge designs the course, and the dog and handler proceed at their own pace through the designated stations. Scoring is not as rigorous as with traditional obedience. Level I classes are done with the dog on leash. Level II classes are done off-leash, including at least one jump. The judge says nothing during the performance, which lasts from the time the dog and handler cross the starting line until they cross the finish line.

Agility

Agility is the ultimate fun sport for Boxers. It will give your dog confidence and keep you fit. It is also one of the most exciting canine sports for spectators. The dog follows cues from the handler through a timed obstacle course, which includes jumps, tunnels, weave poles, A-frames, and seesaws. It is extremely fun and provides vigorous exercise, so the team gets in good shape. A strong bond also develops between dog and owner. Agility is now the fastest-growing dog sport in the United States.

The Standard Class has the dog negotiating obstacles such as the dog walk, A-frame, and seesaw. The next course is Jumpers with Weaves, which, as the name implies, has the dog going over various jumps and through tunnels and weave poles. Both classes offer increasing levels of difficulty to earn Novice, Open, Excellent, and Master titles.

Watching a happy Boxer at the top level run through the course is incredibly exciting. You can sense his eagerness and see his emotions in his face: "Let's go! I can do it!" He charges through the course as fast as he can, working his heart out. When he gets past the finish line, his owner says "Good boy!" and the dog leaps into the air with joy.

You can start agility training with your puppy at home by purchasing a child's play tunnel at a toy store. Other agility equipment can be improvised. You need a low platform to teach *pause*. The dog has to stop on the pause box for a five-second wait, either sitting or lying down, so it incorporates simple obedience commands.

All successful competitors say that training in agility helps build a Boxer's confidence in all areas of his life. It can even prepare him to feel confident and outgoing in the breed ring.

As in all training, start slowly. Introduce your dog to each obstacle. Make the tunnel really short and going through it a game. Use treats to lure him through. He will soon think running through the tunnel is a great game.

One owner gives this advice: "I have trained two Boxers in agility and am working on my third. My first advice is to be careful with the jumps. I had one Boxer tear a ligament while playing at the beach. This shortened his career, even after TPLO surgery. He is a great instructors' dog, though— very careful and thorough with every exercise."

Highly successful competitors start their puppies early. The time spent training your Boxer can be enriching and fun for you both. It enhances the bond that develops between the puppy and his person.

The World of Dog Shows

Dog shows were invented so that experts could select the best specimens of a breed. Most dog shows in the United States are held under the supervision of the American Kennel Club, the largest nonprofit purebred dog registry in the nation. The AKC was established in 1884 to promote the breeding and exhibiting of purebred dogs. The Boxer was recognized as a breed by the AKC in 1904.

FYI: The American Boxer Club

Every year, the American Boxer Club holds a specialty show at which more than 600 Boxers are entered. Regional Boxer clubs also have large entries. These shows are the place to see good Boxers and mingle with Boxer lovers. The American Boxer Club's website (*americanboxerclub.org*) contains information about upcoming specialty shows.

Boxers who are healthy, sound, and move with great ease can win points toward their championship. As excellent representatives of the breed, these dogs are the ones breeders choose to create the next generation.

The standard gives the definition of what the general appearance of a Boxer should be: "The ideal Boxer is a medium-sized, square-built dog of good substance with short back, strong limbs, and short, tight-fitting coat. His well-developed muscles are clean, hard, and appear smooth under taut skin. His movements denote energy. The gait is firm yet elastic, the stride free and ground-covering, and the carriage proud. Developed to serve as guard, working, and companion dog, he combines strength and agility with

elegance and style. His expression is alert and his temperament steadfast and tractable."

Dog shows vary widely in size. The average AKC dog show has 1,000 entries, but some, such as those held in January in Palm Springs, California, or in March in Louisville, Kentucky, have almost 4,000 dogs of all breeds entered.

People participate in dog shows because it's a fun way to spend time with their dogs. Knowledgeable breeders like to get the judge's opinion of their breeding stock. They want to see how their dogs measure up against others. Exhibitors show because it gives them a chance to be around like-minded people, people who are devoted to dogs and like to talk endlessly about them.

Showing dogs is a wonderful family sport. The thrill of competition is combined with the pleasure of seeing lots of beautiful dogs. Junior Showmanship competition is held for young handlers between the ages of 10 to 18.

You can join clubs in order to spend even more time talking about and doing things with dogs. The AKC has 5,000 member clubs. Go to the AKC website (*www.akc.org*), to find a club in your area.

How do dog shows work? A dog show is basically an elimination contest. Winning dogs go on to the next level until they are defeated. The last undefeated dog at the day's end is Best in Show.

At a dog show, your Boxer can be entered in a class specific to his sex and age: Puppy Class, Twelve to Eighteen Months, Novice, Bred by Exhibitor, Amateur Owner-Handler, American-bred, and Open. The winners of each class come back and compete for Winners. Once all males and all females have been judged, champions enter the ring to compete for Best of Breed, also referred to as Specials class.

How does a dog become a champion? A dog must win a total of fifteen points under at least three different judges. Included in these points must be at least two major wins, won under different judges. A major is a win of 3, 4, or 5 points. The number of dogs in the competition determines the number of points awarded. The AKC changes the point schedules annually, but the schedule of points is always spelled out in the show catalog.

Find out where dog shows are being held in the events calendar of the AKC *Gazette*, at the website *www.infodog.com*, or at the websites of any of the dog show superintendents.

Fun Facts

Boxers in the Westminster Dog Show

Boxers have won the Working Group at the Westminster Kennel Club Dog Show 23 times, far more often than any other of the 26 Working breeds. Boxers have placed in the Working Group 47 times. Boxers won Best in Show at Westminster four times, which puts them in a tie with Doberman Pinschers. Only English Springer Spaniels, Wire Fox Terriers, and Scottish Terriers, have won more Westminster Bests in Show than Boxers.

Leash Training

1 Start by snapping the leash on your Boxer puppy's collar and letting him drag it. This will give him a feel for the weight of the leash on his neck. Next, pick up the leash, but don't pull on it. Instead, *you* follow *him*. He may feel confused at first, but Boxers are so smart, he'll soon get used to having you there.

2 Next, call him to you. When he comes, back up and start walking so the two of you are going in the same direction. Reward him with a treat for any progress at all, even if he goes only a few steps. Pet and praise. Then lure him forward and reward with a treat again. Remember, the two of you are having fun. Use your voice to tell him what a clever fellow he is. If he wants to go in a different direction, follow. Then gently ask him to follow you again.

3 If he feels confused, your Boxer may sit down and refuse to move at all. In that case, pick him up and carry him for a few steps. Then put him down and urge him to walk back with you. Boxer puppies are a lot better at going back to their homes than they are at leaving them.

4 Walking on a leash means walking quietly by your side. If he pulls ahead, dragging you, turn around and walk in the opposite direction. Praise him when he walks by your side. If he surges forward, turn again. Boxer babies grow up to be big and strong, so be sure to start this lesson as soon as you get him.

The Sit Command

1 Move your Boxer puppy so he's standing with his back to a corner. Then hold a treat just above his head. Keep your hand closed around the treat and guide him into a sitting position. As soon as his butt hits the ground, give him the treat. You want him to make the connection, "When my butt hits the ground, I get the treat."

2 Repeat the maneuver several times, always remembering to give him the treat instantly when he sits. Three or four times is enough. Then tell him how brilliant he is and what fun it is to work with him. Here's the important point: no more treats until you repeat the exercise. He needs to know that he is *earning* his treats. They do not randomly appear; they appear when he performs the correct action.

3 Training this way is so much fun that he may come to you and sit. Praise him and get out a treat, because he has made an important cognitive leap, connecting his action with the reward.

4 Add the verbal signal "*Sit!*" When he reliably responds, which will take a few days of training, give him the treat only when you request the behavior.

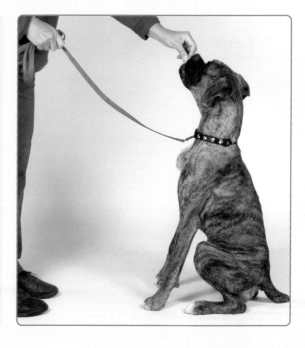

The Stay Command

1 Have him sit beside you, and then say *"Stay"* while holding your palm in a "stop" signal in front of his face. If he gets up, simply put him back in position and start over. Wait for a few seconds, and then say *"Okay!"* Give him the treat.

2 After he's doing this reliably, do it again except this time, pivot so you're standing facing him. Your Boxer will give you that adorable quizzical look, as if to say, "What are you doing?" Wait for a few seconds, then reward him and say *"Okay!"*

3 Next, have him *"sit"* and *"stay"* and back up one step. When he tries to get up to follow you, move toward him and push him back into position.

4 Gradually increase the distance between you. Slowly increase the amount of time he has to stay. Only when he is totally reliable in the *sit/stay* should you introduce mild distractions. This should take at least two weeks and maybe a month. Then practice in other locations and with a longer leash.

Chapter Eight

Grooming

A Boxer requires very little grooming. Boxers are catlike in their desire to be clean. They will spend long minutes carefully licking off dirt and dust from their paws. However, it's a good idea to spend some time grooming your dog, either every day or every week. It helps you monitor his health and well-being. Boxers love the attention and the chance to be with you, and they usually love the soft feel of the brush. Those few minutes become quality time between the two of you. You'll learn to appreciate his good condition. He'll learn to listen better and bond more closely with you. Try giving him vigorous exercise before the grooming session. A Boxer full of energy and eager to get out for a walk finds it hard to hold still.

The Wash and Wear Dog

One lovely thing about your Boxer is that he is naturally clean. He loves to groom himself. His legs shine from being licked. If you don't clean his feet when he comes in from playing, he's happy to lie on his bed and clean them himself.

The Boxer's coat is short and has a Teflon-like quality that repels dirt. He has no undercoat. Sometimes Boxers are advertised as "non-shedding" but that's not true. Those very short hairs will shed, but you generally only see the white ones, and then only when you give your dog a good hug while wearing a black sweater.

Keep a towel by the door so you can ask him to wait and sit while you clean his muddy feet. You'll be amazed at the amount of dirt even a small Boxer foot can hold. Boxer lovers are constantly sweeping up, but it's a small price to pay for their lovely company.

Training for Grooming

If you start to familiarize your puppy with grooming procedures from his first days in your house, you won't have any problems. He'll know what you're doing and love it. However, if you decide to skip this step, you'll find you have a big adult Boxer who is frightened of being put on a table and will struggle and whine to get free. You'll also have trouble getting him to stand still for an examination at the veterinarian's office.

SHOPPING LIST

Grooming Supplies

Everything you need for grooming:

- ✔ Soft brush or grooming glove
- ✔ Nail clippers and/or nail grinder
- ✔ Styptic powder
- ✔ Ear cleaner
- ✔ Cotton swabs
- ✔ Vitamin E oil
- ✔ Flea comb
- ✔ Towel
- ✔ Dog shampoo
- ✔ Petroleum jelly
- ✔ Toothbrush and toothpaste

Therefore, don't skip this step! From the first day, put him up on a table, hold him there, and talk to him. Run your hands over his body. He'll wonder why he has to be up there and may be scared of the height. But he will easily get over it if you stroke him and give him some high-quality treats, like pieces of meat or cheese. At first, keep him there just for a minute, then put him down. He'll feel relieved and seem to think, "Well, that wasn't so bad."

Do it again the next day. It will take about three days to get him comfortable with being up on the table.

Next, introduce him to the brush. Show it to him and let him sniff it. Gently let it touch his body so he knows what it feels like. Over the next day, show him all the things you plan to use on him: flea comb, cotton swabs, towels, and nail clippers. Letting him examine the grooming items first will build his trust.

If he seems scared of anything you show him, pull it back a little so it's further from him. The idea is, "You're afraid of this brush? Okay, I'll move it away. Are you afraid of it if it's a few inches away from you? Yes? Okay, I'll move it to the end of the table. Now you are not afraid of it. Here, eat this treat while you think about it. You can watch it and see that it is not scary. Let's move it an inch closer to you. That's right, it's not scary. Have another treat."

Work in baby steps to desensitize him from being afraid. Every time you use a tool on him, respect him by showing it to

Fun Facts

Military dogs are brushed at least twice a day. Young dog handlers are taught from the start to take their brushes with them everywhere. When the dog takes a break from sniffing for explosives or sentry duty, the handler gets out the brush and gives him a good grooming. It's a relaxing few minutes that both enjoy. It eases the stress of the job, makes the dog feel good, and increases the bond between dog and handler.

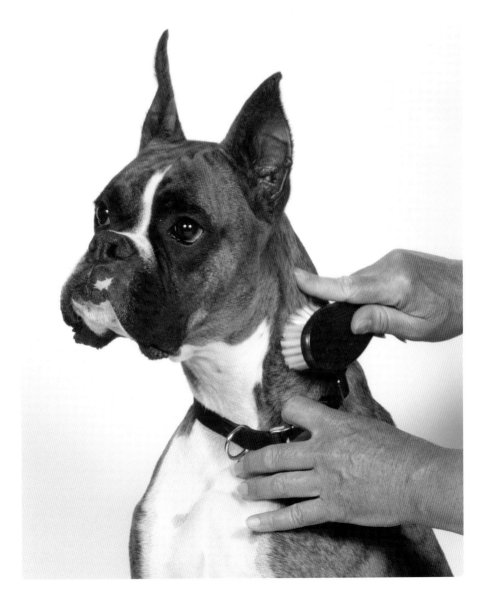

him. If he's afraid, move it away and work in baby steps to bring it back. Again, this is an exercise in building trust.

When he's fine with being on the table, have him sit while you go over him, and then stand. Use this time to gently handle his feet. Dogs don't like having their feet touched, so you'll need to spend a little time on it. Work in baby steps, touching his feet for only a second at first. Then work up to three seconds, then five, and longer.

The face is next. At first, no Boxer likes his face fooled with. But it's important for him to get used to this. Use your fingers to gently touch and rub his skull, cheeks, and muzzle. Practice this when the two of you are relaxing and watching television. Get him to see that having his head handled is normal, and even pleasant.

The teeth will take patience on your part. Dogs find it shocking that you want to look in their mouths. The first step is to rub meat on one finger and slip the finger under his jowls until you can touch his teeth. He won't allow this at first. You'll have to get him used to touching the edge of his lip and then a quick little rub in his mouth with your finger, working up to letting you lift his lip and look at this teeth.

A grooming table—a heavy metal table with a nonslip surface—is a great tool for grooming training. It makes it easy to put your Boxer at eye level so you can examine him. A metal arm can be attached with a noose to hold him still, which is useful when cutting his nails. Grooming tables can be purchased at pet stores or from kennel suppliers online. If you don't have a grooming table, use a sturdy, stable table for this purpose.

Coat

Use a soft brush or grooming glove to go over his whole body, knocking off any stray dirt. You can even use a towel or rag. Boxer skin is sensitive, so don't use a stiff brush and don't press too hard.

A young dog's body should be shiny and smooth. While you're cleaning him, check for any bumps, bare patches, or scrapes. If he's been roughhousing or ran into a fence or tree, he could have minor cuts. Clean any cuts and apply antibacterial cream the first day. If he has a scar that's trying to heal, you can help it along with vitamin E oil. Use your finger, a towel, or a cotton swab to dab it directly on the blemish.

Boxers don't have deep wrinkles like Bulldogs or Pugs, but it's still important to check his facial wrinkles by running a towel or cotton swab over them. If his nose is dry and crusty, apply a dab of petroleum jelly to soften it. Boxers do shed, but if you groom once a week to remove the dead hair, you will see less of it on the furniture. Boxer coats repel dirt, so it's not necessary to bathe him often. However, if he's rubbed himself in some awful odor, as dogs love to do, it's time for a bath. The easiest place is most likely

CHECKLIST

Grooming

When grooming, be sure to check:

✔ Coat	✔ Eyes	✔ Ears	✔ Teeth
✔ Feet	✔ Wrinkles	✔ Nails	

your own bathtub. In the summer, a bath can be given outdoors. Another possibility is to sponge-bathe him on the grooming table.

Pet stores are full of dog shampoos, so you have a wide choice, from flea shampoos to oatmeal shampoos to old-fashioned formulas. Pour the shampoo on his back and mix with water to lather and spread all over his body. As soon as he's out of the tub, he'll shake his whole body and water drops will fly everywhere. Use a towel to get him dry.

Eyes

Boxer eyes are usually clean and bright. Hold your dog's head in your hands and look directly into the eyes. If you do this almost every day, you'll quickly notice if anything is wrong, and he will become accustomed to being handled. Clean any tears or discharge from the wrinkle in front of the eye. If dirt builds up there, it can become irritated.

Canine ophthalmology specialists handle canine eye problems. Veterinarians with this medical specialty often have offices together with other veterinary specialists. Some make visits to local veterinary offices on a regular basis.

Ears

Whether your dog's ears are cropped or uncropped, they need occasional attention to keep them clean. Use a cotton swab with a small amount of hydrogen peroxide or an ear-cleansing solution to clean the inside of the ear. If you notice a buildup of dark or red wax and a bad smell, it could indicate the presence of ear mites. For that, he'll need a trip to the veterinarian for prescription medication.

It's important to get him used to having his ears cleaned in case he ever gets an infection. It is very hard to hold down a full-grown Boxer who doesn't want his ears touched. It's better to get him accustomed to this while he's young.

One Boxer owner has a clever way of keeping her Boxer occupied while she cleans his ears: "I've started putting peanut butter on the end of his nose so he'll be preoccupied with licking it off and I can clean his ears in peace."

Boxer ear cleaning goes a lot easier if you have a second person to help. The assistant can hold a Kong filled with peanut butter or some other distraction in front of him while you use the cotton swab to wipe out his ears.

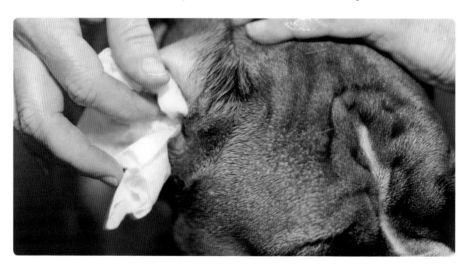

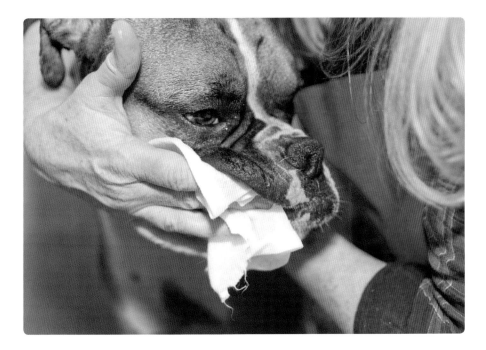

Teeth

Boxers love to chew. Encourage your dog to do so with chew toys made of hard rubber or rawhide. Nylon and rope chew toys are good, too. These materials rub against his teeth and gums, stimulating the blood supply and knocking off tartar. Toys will keep his teeth clean.

Boxers are reluctant to let you brush their teeth. You'll need to go slow to accustom him to staying still while you do it. Use a soft human toothbrush or get one from a pet store. Pet toothpaste comes in beef and chicken flavors, or you can use baking soda mixed with water. An even easier method of teeth cleaning is to use gauze to rub his teeth, which is less invasive than a toothbrush. You can also buy a finger brush that is specially made for dog dental cleanings.

Tartar buildup contributes to tooth decay and bad breath. If he has significant bad breath or visible tooth decay, your veterinarian will need to clean the teeth while he's under anesthesia.

Nails

No dog likes his nails cut, but it is necessary for his well-being. Long nails will cause his feet to splay and make it hard to stand on slippery surfaces. His nails should not make clicking sounds on the floor. They should not be pointy and sharp. They should not scratch and gouge your skin when he touches you. For his health and safety, his nails need to be kept short.

There are four toes with nails on each foot, and sometimes another nail called a dewclaw a little way up the inside of the front leg. The dewclaws may be removed when the puppy is three to five days old.

Before you cut his nails, either have someone hold him or put him on the grooming table and secure him with the grooming noose. Using dog nail clippers, clip just the tip of the nail. Be careful not to cut into the quick, the vein in the center of the nail. The quick is usually easily visible in a white nail but impossible to see if the nails are black. If you cut the quick, it will bleed, but just a little. Everyone nips the quick accidentally sometimes. If you keep the nail trimmed, it keeps the quick back.

If the toenail bleeds after being cut, press a pinch of styptic powder to it and hold for three seconds. This is not a serious injury, so don't panic. The bleeding will stop easily. You will never get a Boxer to enjoy having his nails cut, so just do it as quickly as you can. Praise him and give treats when you're finished. If you trim the tips every week or so, the nail will stay short.

The grinder is another tool that makes it even easier to keep his nails short. The new, battery-powered grinders make very little noise. First, acclimate the dog to the grinder by holding it in front of him. Turn it on and off, letting him see that it is

Helpful Hints

When grinding his nails, hold your Boxer's foot gently. It's easy to put too much pressure on the foot, causing him to try to pull away.

BE PREPARED! Skunk Smell Remover

Boxers who live in the country may one day encounter a skunk, with bad results. When frightened, the skunk sprays the dog with his horrible smell. Shampoo will not remove it.

To get rid of the smell, put the Boxer in a bathtub and cover him with tomato juice. You'll need at least 4 quarts of tomato juice for this task. Try to leave the juice on him for a few minutes to allow the chemicals to do their work. Then rinse him thoroughly.

Here's another home recipe for removing skunk smell: Get a bucket and mix 1 quart of hydrogen peroxide with ¼ cup baking soda and 2 tablespoons of detergent. Wash the dog with this mixture while it is still foaming.

not going to hurt him. Speak calmly to him. Give him treats. Next, with the grinder turned off, gently rub him on the leg with it. You are deconditioning any fear he has, showing him he won't be hurt if the grinder touches him. Boxers are smart and this usually doesn't take long.

With the grinder still off, pick up one foot and touch the nails, praising him and rewarding with treats if he stays still and lets you do it. Then turn it on. The first time the grinder touches his toes might startle him, so reassure him that it's okay. Some Boxers aren't bothered at all by this time, others look on curiously, and others are bored. Those are much better reactions than having a scared Boxer on your hands. Hold one toe and use the grinder gently on one side of the nail, then the other side, then in the center. Several Internet sites offer systematic instructions and videos to show you exactly how to use the grinder.

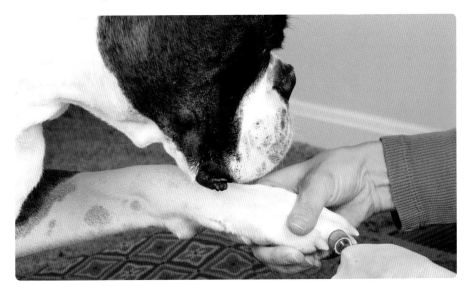

Chapter Nine

The Senior Boxer

It's a sad fact of life that our Boxers grow old. One day they are bouncing puppies, looking to us for play and direction, then rowdy adults, figuring out how to entertain us with their antics. Eventually, you notice the hair on his muzzle beginning to turn gray. He doesn't run as fast to the door when you get home. Maybe he starts to avoid stairs and walks a bit unsteadily through the backyard.

His job was to be your best friend and companion. Now it's your job to notice what hurts him and provide for his comfort in his older days.

The Elderly Boxer

If your dog has arthritis or hip dysplasia and moving is painful, you may need to build a ramp for him to negotiate stairs or to get into the car.

Older dogs may also experience hearing loss. He's not ignoring you; he just can't hear you calling him.

Your older Boxer wants to be warm. Keep a comfortable bed out of drafts. He may be glad for a blanket pulled over him at night. If it's really cold, consider a coat. There are many different types on the market. For outdoor walks, a good choice is one with a nylon outer shell and soft inner liner, designed like a horse blanket, with Velcro fastenings. These coats are waterproof and easy to get on and off.

Indoors, coats made of warm fleece and polyester materials will warm him. Some people like their dogs to wear sweaters. The only downside to sweaters is that they are hard to get on and off, as you have to pull the dog's front legs through the armholes.

Behavioral Changes

Older dogs love a stable routine at home. They are happy to nap all day while the family is at work. Most are trustworthy because they don't soil the house or chew furniture. Other older dogs may show behavioral changes.

These are generally the result of physical illness or weakness, which make them less able to handle stress. Look for signs that your older dog is feeling stressed, such as increased panting.

Separation Anxiety

Some older dogs acquire separation anxiety, even though they got over it long ago as puppies. He's worrying about how long you'll be gone and how long he'll feel alone. If his vision is fading or some hearing is lost, he may feel more anxious when you leave. Treat separation anxiety in an older dog the same way as in a younger one. First, exercise before you leave will definitely help relax him. After a long walk, he'll be happy for a long nap. If possible, take him for a walk or throw balls for him before you leave.

Teach him to calm down by refreshing his training in all the commands he knows. When you are in the house with him, ask him to lie down on his bed and stay while you are in the same room, within his sight. If he can relax when you are at home, there's a better chance he can relax when you're gone. Ask for the *down-stay* when you leave the house.

A dog with separation anxiety is always overly jubilant when his owner returns, so don't reward that. Just a pat on the head and a greeting shows him that your comings and goings are no big deal and certainly no reason to be anxious.

As with youngsters, a toy with a treat inside may keep him occupied and associate your leaving with something good. If you're gone for long hours, you may need to get someone to come during the day to let him out. Older dogs can't hold it as long as they could when they were younger, and he may be uncomfortable. Spayed bitches often develop "spay incontinence" when they get older, so be mindful of this as well.

If he's anxious about being left alone, get out the crate. Curled up in his crate with a comfortable cushion, your dog may feel safer and calmer.

If he's really anxious, a veterinary medication called Clomicalm may give him some relief from anxiety. However, medication alone will not solve the problem, nor is it a long-term answer. It's simply a way to get him to relax and realize everything is okay. You will still need to use some of the other behavioral steps described here.

Breed Needs

To keep your senior Boxer comfortable:

- Give him a comfortable bed in a draft-free area.
- Try to keep his bed and food in areas where he won't have to go up and down stairs.
- If he has to use stairs, see if a ramp is easier for him.
- Pay close attention to his health, particularly problems such as arthritis and cataracts.
- Check his dental health. Gum disease, tartar buildup, and tooth loss may bother older dogs and can be treated by a veterinarian.
- Make sure he's eating well. Raw meat and bones may help stimulate his appetite.

Aggressive Behavior

Occasionally, owners are shocked to find that an older dog has become aggressive, when he never was before. There is probably a medical reason for the aggression. If he has painful arthritis or gums, he won't have patience with roughhousing and may be telling another dog or a child to stop hurting him. Your veterinarian will need to diagnose and relieve his condition.

Additionally, dogs who lose part of their vision and some of their hearing may become easily startled. They don't see or hear familiar people and may think they are growling at a stranger.

Older dogs who have been completely housetrained for years may start having accidents in the house. Boxers are very clean and will endure all they can in order not to soil their home. Most likely, there is a medical reason for accidents, such as colitis, inflammatory bowel disease, bladder stones, bladder infections, inflammation of the prostate, Cushing's disease, diabetes, spay incontinence, prostate trouble, or kidney or liver disease. At least a third of spayed females, as previously mentioned, suffer from spay incontinence, when the muscles are not able to prevent leakage from the bladder.

Disorientation

If your dog seems confused and disoriented, he may be suffering from canine cognitive dysfunction. This is common in dogs over age 10, just as similar problems crop up for older humans. He may not recognize friends or family members, spend a lot of time staring into space, and be inattentive to things he used to care about, like helping Mom cook dinner in the kitchen.

But remember, with lots of patience and attention, and your veterinarian's help, your dog's older years can still be a quality time of life.

Mealtime for Seniors

Because he's slowing down, your senior Boxer needs fewer calories. Cut back on the amount he eats if he gets a little chubby. When you pat his side, you should be able to feel his ribs. Statistics now show that Americans are letting their dogs get as chubby as they are. This is especially bad for your older dog, who doesn't need any extra stress on his joints. Your older Boxer should be kept in the lean, athletic condition he had as a youngster.

Senior dogs need high-quality protein. Either feed him less of his regular food, or try one of the kibbles made especially for older dogs. Senior foods are designed to put less stress on the kidneys. They may also contain glucosamine and chondroitin to ease the pain of arthritis. Seniors are predisposed to form dental tartar on their teeth, so senior food may contain sodium tripolyphosphates, which reduce tartar deposits by binding salivary calcium. Antioxidants such as those found in vitamins C and E, beta-carotene, and selenium stimulate the immune system.

What you should not do is feed a "low fat" or "lite" food, which reduces the essential fats your dog needs for good health. Because older Americans get heavy and look for non-fat or low-fat products, they think their dogs need the same thing. But this is far from the truth, especially for Boxers, who don't tend to store fat. Boxers need fats to help burn protein, contribute to their energy level, ensure healthy skin and coat, and keep the heart muscles pumping in good shape.

Notice how often you refill his water bowl. Excessive water drinking and urination may be a sign of kidney disease, diabetes, or another life-threatening condition.

Health Concerns

Many elderly Boxers have few health concerns and live full lives. But to ensure your senior Boxer stays healthy, he'll need a complete inspection each week. You can do this as a grooming session, using a soft brush to go over his entire body. Frequent grooming can help prevent some skin conditions. Grooming also means cutting his nails, which is really crucial for an older dog. Long nails will cause his feet to be pushed apart and hurt. He'll slip on wood or tile floors. Long nails will make the pain of arthritis even worse. So keep those nails comfortably short.

While you're grooming, inspect him for any unusual lumps or growths. An alternate possibility is to examine him on the couch or bed while the two of you are watching television. Very often, lumps and growths are benign. But if they are malignant, removal at the earliest stage is the best course of action.

Arthritis

Arthritis is a common problem for all older dogs. Your senior Boxer may move stiffly and slowly, particularly when getting up after a nap. Nonsteroidal pain medication can greatly improve the quality of life for an arthritic Boxer. Stiffness and pain when moving can be signs of other problems, as well, such as Lyme disease or a spinal ailment. Pay attention to your older friend and notice if he's having trouble walking.

Dental Problems

The Boxer is prone to developing gingival hyperplasia, an overgrowth of gum tissue. It's not dangerous, but it can cause tooth decay and bleeding from the gums. Your veterinarian will show you how to brush your dog's teeth, which can help prevent the condition.

Preventative Health Care

To enhance the quality of life for senior Boxers, veterinarians recommend a proactive approach, rather than waiting until your Boxer is suffering from an age-related illness. Instead of yearly visits, he may need twice-yearly exams. Guidelines published by the American Animal Hospital Association recommend that dogs undergo laboratory tests beginning at middle age. The following tests are recommended:

- A complete blood count (CBC) test measures levels of red and white blood cells and platelets, an increase or decrease of which may signal a health problem.
- Urinalysis is helpful in detecting kidney problems, diabetes, urinary tract infections, and other conditions.
- A serum chemistry panel measures the levels of electrolytes (potassium, sodium, and magnesium), the elements calcium and phosphorus, and certain enzymes, providing information on the functioning of your Boxer's pancreas, kidneys, and liver.
- A parasite evaluation may be necessary, despite the parasite prevention program you've had him on all his life. As your dog ages, your veterinarian may want to do a fecal exam to check for disease-causing parasites, such as roundworm, hookworm, and whipworm, and to look for bleeding in the intestinal tract or a pancreatic illness.

Depending on your pet's particular condition, your veterinarian may recommend other tests, such as X-rays. You know your Boxer best. By keeping a close watch on his general attitude, appetite, thirst, and elimination, you are his best hope for a long and happy life.

FYI: Boxer Groups

If your Boxer begins to develop health problems, one source of information and emotional support are the Boxer groups on the Internet. They offer the chance to dialogue with other Boxer owners about the problems they've encountered and the solutions. Most longtime Boxer owners have had an old one. It is comforting to find that others have dealt with the same problems, which can feel overwhelming when you're facing them alone.

Senior Rescue

Sadly, many older dogs are dropped off at shelters, some because they require surgery or veterinary care that is too expensive for their owners. They may have erratic heartbeats, thyroid glands that are not producing enough hormones, or arthritic joints that cause them to wobble.

There is not much call in shelters and rescue operations for older dogs. People want the cute, bouncy puppy, under a year old, all eagerness and fun. Older dogs aren't going to live as long, may have health problems, and may be more trouble to own.

But an older Boxer can also be uniquely rewarding. One woman who adopted an elderly Boxer recalls, "She was the perfect dog. I never intended to adopt an older dog, but she was so sweet, I took her home. I'm so glad I could do something for her by making her life comfortable for her last months. She brought an extra element to my life. My world was richer because of her."

When you are looking to adopt, don't write off the older dogs. They may not have many years left, but there's no limit on the amount of love they have to give.

What Boxers Do for Seniors

Owning a dog is a wonderful way for elderly citizens to fill a void in their lives, especially if they live alone. Dogs can greatly improve their quality of life.

The best dog for an elderly person may be an elderly Boxer. They are less active and more willing to take long naps. They are loving and sweet without being demanding. The elderly Boxer provides unconditional love and admiration. They are good company when no one else has time to visit.

Dr. Lynette Hart, director of the University of California/Davis Center for Animal Alternatives, writes in her article "The Role of Pets in Enhancing Human Well-being: Effects for Older People" that a dog can bring down

157

blood pressure, reduce the heart rate, induce the relaxation response, and get elderly people up for exercise.

Dr. Hart is also an outspoken advocate of therapy dogs. "The most important role of dogs as therapy dogs," Dr. Hart says, "is that dogs are social lubricants. A dog comes visiting patients in the hospital, goes up to their beds, and they pat him on the head. They tell the owner about the dog they used to have. The owner tells them the dog's favorite things to eat. There's a social interaction, and then the dog team goes on their way. The patient's blood pressure goes down, they feel calmer and more relaxed, and they're thinking about something other than their illness."

Dr. Hart says doing therapy dog work is also good for the owners: "They get to spend time with their dog, instead of leaving the dog home all the time, which they are usually feeling guilty about. They're giving the dog a job. That's very appealing. That's why it works, because the human accompanying the dog gets a lot out of it."

In the following studies, scientists have established beyond doubt the therapeutic value of dogs for the elderly.

Helpful Hints

- A study at the Mayo Clinic Medical School found that 12 months after suffering heart attacks, 90 percent of those who owned pets survived, as opposed to 70 percent of those without pets.
- In England, Cambridge University researchers discovered that, within a month of taking a dog into their homes, elderly owners reported a highly significant reduction in minor ailments.

An organization called Pets for the Elderly Foundation matches seniors with dogs and pays the adoption fees. The general manager of the organization, Susan Kurowski, says, "Those who are responsible for a pet are likely to take better care of themselves, because they feel someone is counting on them." Check out Pets for the Elderly by visiting the foundation's website at *www.petsfortheelderly.org*.

- A Japanese Animal Hospital Association study of people over 65 found that pet owners made 30 percent fewer visits to doctors than those who had no pet. At least part of the reason for this is that dogs, with their steady presence, help us reduce our state of arousal, which reduces blood pressure.
- The Delta Society, whose mission is to improve human health through service and therapy animals, has found that the benefits of dog ownership to senior citizens are extraordinary. A study in the *Journal of the American Geriatrics Society* confirmed the group's view that elderly pet owners are more active, cope better with stress, and have lower blood pressure than those without pets.

As John Lipp, president of the San Francisco organization Pets Are Wonderful Support, says, "If pet ownership was a medication, it would sell off the shelves. But the kind of good feelings the elderly get from owning a pet can't be bottled."

Bringing in a Young Companion

One decision that the owners of older Boxers often ponder is whether to bring a young Boxer into the family. Often, having a youngster around is invigorating for the older guy. A young Boxer gives the older one a chance to play and cuddle. Older Boxers generally like showing younger ones the ropes. A definite plus is that dogs learn from each other. The young guy will

pick up the rules from watching what his elder does. Housetraining and property boundaries are easier to learn with a mentor.

Some owners worry that a younger dog may be so energetic that the situation becomes stressful for the older one. That problem can be avoided by taking your time to choose the perfect companion. A crazy, undisciplined puppy might not be the best choice. But if you keep looking, you'll come across one who is quieter and more easy-going, ready to look before leaping into trouble. You know your senior dog better than anyone. Consider his age, health, and energy level. Make sure he doesn't have any hip or joint trouble that would keep him from being more active.

Generally, getting a friendly younger companion for an older dog has benefits that outweigh any downsides. They'll keep each other company, be more active, and get into better physical condition. Dogs who live together bond deeply. The younger dog will likely grieve with you when the sad day comes and your older Boxer is gone.

When to Say Good-Bye

One of life's most heart-wrenching decisions is having to put your elderly Boxer to sleep. It would be so much easier for us if they simply went to sleep on their beds one night. Unfortunately, that's often not the case. Sometimes the other organs are failing, yet the heart keeps on beating.

How do you know when time is right? You don't want your beloved pal of many years to suffer. If he can't stand, he won't be able to go outdoors and will be forced to lie in his own waste, something your dog would never want to do. Maybe you get by this problem by carrying him out several times a day and constantly washing his bedding. Owners have been known to do this for months or even years because they can't face losing their beloved pal.

Is he eating? If he can still look forward to dinnertime, he still has some joy in his life. But when he can no longer eat, his body is shutting down.

Some people feel they know when it's time. Others prefer that the veterinarian make the decision. You'll need the support of family and friends that day.

BE PREPARED! Boxer Burial

One of the sad things about dog ownership is that you are likely to outlive your pet. You may want to give some thought in advance to your Boxer's final resting place. Many people bury their dogs in the backyard, under a favorite tree. Cremation is now common for pets, so that their ashes can be sprinkled in a special spot. There are also pet cemeteries near many towns. Check out places and options in your area to decide what's best for you.

When we choose to travel in the company of a canine, we enter a relationship unlike the ones we have with our human friends. While we may live as long as a century, a Boxer's life will be about a decade. Those who have never lived through the joys and challenges of owning a Boxer may not comprehend our willingness to give our love to another eager puppy, with the full knowledge that ten years down the line, our hearts will be broken again. Those who have spent time in a Boxer's company know how small a price it is to pay for what we receive. Our grief at his passing is deep, but the joy of living with a Boxer is immeasurable.

Resources

Books and Articles

Becker, Marty, DVM. "Caring for Older Pets and Their Families." *Firstline* August/September 1998: 28–30.

Bernikow, Louise. *Bark If You Love Me.* Chapel Hill, NC: Algonquin Books of Chapel Hill, 2000.

——. *Dreaming in Libro.* Washington, DC: Da Capo Press, 2005.

Billinghurst, Ian, DVM. *Give Your Dog a Bone: The Practical Commonsense Way to Feed Dogs for a Long Healthy Life.* Self-published, 1993.

Carlson, Delbert G., DVM, and James M. Giffin, MD. *Dog Owner's Home Veterinary Handbook.* Hoboken, NJ: Howell Book House, 1980. This is a good first aid book to have on hand in an emergency, or simply to answer a question about your dog's health. A comprehensive dog care guide, it includes lots of medical details.

Denlinger, Milo. *The Complete Boxer.* New York: Howell Book House, 1969. This is a collection of essays from some of the most knowledgeable Boxer breeders of the early 1900s. Photos and charts demonstrate the development of the breed.

Lonsdale, Tom, DVM. *Work Wonders: Feed Your Dog Raw Meaty Bones.* Wenatchee, WA: Dogwise Publishing, 2005.

Royal Canin. *The Boxer: Best Balance of Nutrients for Boxers.* Introduction by Pascal Jouannet. This booklet, available from the Royal Canin dog food company, summarizes many health studies done on Boxers around the world.

Sakson, Sharon. *Paws & Effect: The Healing Power of Dogs.* New York: Spiegel & Grau, 2009.

——. *Paws to Protect: Dogs Saving Lives and Restoring Hope.* New York: Alyson Books, 2009.

——. *Paws and Reflect: A Special Bond Between Man and Dog.* New York: Alyson Books, 2007.

Stockmann, Friederun. *My Life with Boxers.* Translated from the German by Calvin Gruver. This book traces the origins and development of the Boxer breed, written by the breeder who was part of its history. To view the table of contents, go to *http://web.stcloudstate.edu/cdgruver/_private/index.htm.*

Volpe, Stanley U. *This Is the Boxer.* TFH Publications, Inc., 1964. This old book is a treasury of Boxer history, with advice about showing and breeding from a Boxer expert.

Books on Training

Don't Shoot the Dog!: The New Art of Teaching and Training by Karen Pryor. Bantam Books, 1999. This book helps owners understand how dogs learn and explains how to use that knowledge to train them. The author teaches how to house-train and put an end to undesirable behavior. More than a training book, it also delves deeply into animal psychology.

How to Be Your Dog's Best Friend by the Monks of New Skete. Little, Brown and Co., original edition 1978, update 2002. This step-by-step training manual covers every aspect of dog ownership, including naming the puppy, training with eye contact, establishing the sleeping arrange-ments, and even dealing with pet loneliness. It also explores the deep spiritual connection that is possible between humans and dogs.

The Art of Raising a Puppy by the Monks of New Skete. Little, Brown and Co., 1991. Geared to the new dog owner, this excellent book describes and illustrates the Monks' distinctive approach to dog training.

People, Pooches and Problems: Understanding, Controlling and Correcting Problem Behavior in Your Dog by Job Michael Evans. Howell Book House, 1991. Evans discusses how to develop your leadership role with your dog, as well as how to prevent problems.

The Evans Guide for Housetraining Your Dog. by Job Michael Evans. Macmillan, 1987.

Books on Health

How to Buy and Raise a Good Healthy Dog by Terri Shumsky. Doral Publishing, 2001. This book covers every aspect of caring for a dog, with lots of easy-to-understand details regarding canine health.

The Angell Memorial Animal Hospital Book of Wellness and Preventive Care for Dogs by Darlene Arden. McGraw-Hill, 2004. This sensible book about dog health is full of useful explana-tions of technical terms about dog illnesses.

Dog Owner's Home Veterinary Handbook by Delbert G. Carlson, DVM, and James M. Giffin, MD. Howell Book House, 1980.

Websites

American Boxer Charitable Foundation
www.abcfoundation.org
Foundation whose mission is to raise money to fund research into the health-related issues that face Boxers.

American Kennel Club
www.akc.org
The largest registry for purebred dogs in the United States.

American Kennel Club Canine Health Foundation
www.akcchf.org
The largest nonprofit worldwide foundation to fund health research exclusively for canines.

American Boxer Club
www.americanboxerclub.org

American Boxer Rescue
  Association
www.americanboxerrescue.org

Articles about Boxers by
  Richard Cussons
www.boxersavvy.com

Bergin University
www.berginu.edu
The only accredited university for
dog studies.

Boxer Buddies
www.boxerbuddies.org

Boxer World
www.boxerworld.com

Delta Society
www.deltasociety.org

Legacy Boxer Rescue of
  Dallas-Fort Worth
www.savetheboxers.com

Nationwide Pet Adoption website
www.petfinders.org

New Jersey Boxer Rescue
www.njboxerrescue.com

Orthopedic Foundation for Animals
www.offa.org

Raw Diet for Boxers
www.rawboxers.com

The Healing Power of Dogs
www.healingpowerofdogs.com

Therapy Dogs International
www.tdi-dog.org

University of Pennsylvania School of
  Veterinary Medicine/PennHip
*www.vet.upenn.edu/ResearchCenters/
pennhip/what_is_ph.html*

www.WebVet.com
Answers to veterinary questions.

Index

THE TEAM BEHIND THE *TRAIN YOUR DOG* DVD

Host **Nicole Wilde** is a certified Pet Dog Trainer and internationally recognized author and lecturer. Her books include *So You Want to Be a Dog Trainer* and *Help for Your Fearful Dog* (Phantom Publishing). In addition to working with dogs, Nicole has been working with wolves and wolf hybrids for over fifteen years and is considered an expert in the field.

Host **Laura Bourhenne** is a Professional Member of the Association of Pet Dog Trainers, and holds a degree in Exotic Animal Training. She has trained many species of animals including several species of primates, birds of prey, and many more. Laura is striving to enrich the lives of pets by training and educating the people they live with.

Director **Leo Zahn** is an award winning director/cinematographer/editor of television commercials, movies, and documentaries. He has directed and edited more than a dozen instructional DVDs through the Picture Company, a subsidiary of Picture Palace, Inc., based in Los Angeles.